TODAY WITH ISAIAH

Volume 2

Clifford Hill

The Centre for Biblical and Hebraic Studies

Other books in this series

Today with Jeremiah - Volume 1
Today with Jeremiah - Volume 2
Today with Isaiah - Volume 1

Copyright ' The Centre for Biblical and Hebraic Studies 2001

Published by The Centre for Biblical and Hebraic Studies a ministry of CCM (Charity Number: 1022698)

First published 2001

Unless otherwise indicated, biblical quotes are from the New International Version ' 1973, 1978, 1984 by the International Bible Society.

ISBN: 1-872395 75 9

British Library Cataloguing in Publication Data.
A catalogue record for this book is available from the British Library.

Printed by Cox and Wyman, Reading, England

Manuscript typed by Jean Wolton and Ruth Addington
Proof read by Pam Smith, Val Lockhart and Alyson Perry

Typeset by Andrew Lewis

TODAY WITH ISAIAH

VOLUME 2

FOREWORD

The writings of the Hebrew prophets are for many a little known or even completely unexplored treasury of riches. Even if we did not have the writings of the New Testament and the full revelation of the nature of God in the person of the Messiah, the Lord Jesus Christ, we would still find, in the revelation given through Moses and the prophets, that God had already revealed every aspect of his character. This would finally be demonstrated in the person of a human being who was the word made flesh, the Lord Jesus.

Jesus himself showed clearly that he understood his earthly ministry of revelation and redemption as fulfilment of the Hebrew scriptures, all of which point to him and were intended to prepare the nation of Israel to recognise him when he came, and to understand the purpose for which he had been sent by the Father.

For those who had eyes to see, ears to hear and hearts to understand the witness which the Holy Spirit gave, this was indeed the case; and the writings of the Early Church which we now call the New Testament prove it to be so. The revelation of the person and work of Christ was given as the Spirit of Truth enlightened his disciples with understanding of how he fulfils the prophetic writings.

Despite this, however, throughout its history the Gentile Church has been impoverished by neglect of the prophetic scriptures of which Jesus is the living fulfilment. The inevitable result has been a lack of understanding of many aspects of the character of the God into whose family we have been adopted. We have been like a man who is seeing with only one eye and does not realise that in consequence he is blind to a considerable part of what he should see, nor that what he does perceive is lacking in true perspective. Without a knowledge and understanding of the writings of the Old Testament, we can have only a restricted and often distorted understanding of the New Testament revelation which stands entirely upon the foundations already laid in God's word.

Of all the great Hebrew prophets, none had a broader vision of God's purposes or a deeper revelation of the Father's heart than Isaiah, and it is therefore both a pleasure and a privilege to write a word of introduction to this new volume of devotional studies by Clifford Hill. I have known Clifford for many years as a friend and as a colleague in ministry and often the scripture that 'as iron sharpens iron, so one man sharpens another' (Proverbs 27:17) has been proved true as we have examined the word of God together.

Clifford is a man with a deep love of the word and especially of the writings of the Hebrew prophets, particularly of Isaiah and Jeremiah. The understanding gained from many years of study of their revelation of the character and ways of God, together with his personal expertise in the science of sociology, has equipped him in a unique way to be able to relate the justice and righteousness of God's call to repentance and warnings of judgment to the increasingly depraved and godless society in which we live. Yet at the same time, he has a heart of compassion which identifies readily with God's words of comfort, encouragement and reassurance which were also a vital ingredient in the message of Isaiah.

This series of short devotional studies contains a balance of emphasis upon both these aspects of Isaiah's revelation of the heart of God. I believe that the reader will receive the dual blessing both of deeper insight and understanding of these scriptures and of the Lord's encouragement and comfort to his people which Isaiah was so well able to hear and convey. It is my prayer that this will be the experience of many as they dwell upon the truths which Clifford Hill has underlined in a way which reveals his own depth of understanding, but is at the same time both simple and refreshing to the spirit.

David Noakes
April 2001

PREFACE

Isaiah 40 to 53

These are the most popular chapters in the whole book of Isaiah. For most people they contain some of the best loved passages to be found anywhere in the Bible. Their message is one of hope and confidence in the Lord. They look back to the mighty acts of God in creation and they look forward in faith to the great things that God is going to do. Their whole purpose is to build up trust in the Lord and to direct the people to be looking to the Lord as their Saviour and Provider, their Guide and Protector.

There is a greater proportion of prophecies in the first person singular in these chapters than anywhere else in the writings of the prophets. The prophet here is not simply speaking his own words or offering his own forecast of what is likely to happen in the future. In these passages the prophet is not an author, he is a messenger; he is acting as the mouthpiece of God, reporting what the Lord has declared in his hearing. These pronouncements represent an enormous leap forward in the revelation of God's nature and purposes given to us in Scripture. There are statements here that no human being would dare to make about God such as 'I form the light and create darkness, I bring prosperity and create disaster' (45:7). Inevitably, this raises the question as to whether God is the author of evil as well as good which is one of the questions faced in these studies.

Throughout these chapters the ringing declaration 'I am the Lord, and there is no other' sets the scene for the presentation of God as the sovereign Lord of all creation and the God of history who holds the nations in his hands as 'a drop in a bucket'. The good news presented here is that God was about to bring about the downfall of Babylon and thereby release his people from exile and enable them to go back to Judah. In the build-up to this message the prophet establishes the authority of God and contrasts him with the pagan idols of popular religion in Babylon. These were just blocks of wood and stone and as such were powerless to answer the prayers of their worshippers.

In these chapters God is revealed as the one who has existed since the beginning of time, the one who not only created the world but also set the stars in their places and sustains the universe. 'Before me no god was formed, nor will there be one after me. I, even I, am the Lord, and apart from me there is no saviour' (43:10b-11). It is statements such as these that represent a great advance in theology, in the revelation of God himself.

The purpose of this revelation at this point in history was to prepare the exiles for an understanding of their unique calling as the covenant people of God. Until now the people of Israel had never fully understood why God had called them, as a nation, into a covenant relationship with himself. It was not because they were the most numerous or the nation most favoured by God. His purpose was simply that he needed a nation of people who would be completely devoted to him so that they could be used in a servant capacity. They were to be the means through whom God would reveal himself to the world. Israel was to be a light for the Gentiles. It is this tremendous truth that was revealed to Isaiah of the Exile and is so magnificently presented in the poetry of these chapters.

This section of the book of Isaiah climaxes in what are known as the Servant Songs where the nature of the calling of Israel is revealed. The way is prepared for the idealised Israel in the person of the Messiah the Servant who was destined to suffer. This amazing revelation comes as the climax to the message and shows how God uses suffering redemptively so that the Servant of the Lord becomes the Redeemer of his people and not only of Israel but of all men and women.

Most biblical scholars recognise this central section of the book of Isaiah as finishing at the end of chapter 55. There are strong grounds for accepting this but we have chosen to conclude this volume of studies at the end of chapter 53 partly for logistical reasons but also because the message of the suffering of the Kinsman Redeemer forms a fitting climax to the purposes of God revealed to the prophet of the exile.

Historical Background

The historical background to this central section of Isaiah is set out in 44:24 - 28. *This is what the Lord says - your Redeemer, who formed you in the womb... who says of Jerusalem, 'It shall be inhabited' of the towns of Judah, 'They shall be built,' and of their ruins, 'I will restore them,' .... who says of Cyrus, 'He is my shepherd and will accomplish all that I please; he will say of Jerusalem, "Let it be rebuilt," and of the Temple, "let its foundations be laid".'*

This presents a picture of the land of Judah in a state of desolation with all its major towns and cities destroyed and with Jerusalem, including the Temple, lying in ruins. This was the work of Nebuchadnezzar and the Babylonian army who had invaded Judah during the reign of Zedekiah and the ministry of Jeremiah. After a prolonged siege Jerusalem had fallen and the Babylonian army had systematically razed the city to the ground including destroying the Temple, the palace and all the great houses of Jerusalem. Its walls and gates lay in ruins for all to see the humiliation of a once great city and it remained in this state from 587 BC until Babylon fell to Cyrus the Persian in 539 BC. For more than a generation Jerusalem was virtually uninhabited and a large part of the population of Judah was in exile in Babylon.

Nebuchadnezzar died in 562 BC and throughout his reign the Babylonian empire remained the most powerful empire the world had yet known. The next seven years was a period of uncertainty with three kings in quick succession leading to the reign of Nabonidus, the last king of Babylon who reigned from 556 to 539 BC. Nabonidus worshipped Sin, the moon god, and restored her temple in Haran some 500 miles to the south of Babylon which he established as his capital. This offended the priests of Marduk the official god of Babylon who turned against Nabonidus and played a leading part in influencing the people to welcome Cyrus as a liberator when he eventually marched against Babylon in 539 BC.

Cyrus' rise to power from the small vassal kingdom of Anshan in what is now Southern Iran (biblical Elam) was quite meteoric. Around 550 BC he expanded his territory by capturing Ecbatana which caused Croesus the king of Lydia to feel threatened. Croesus, after consulting the oracle and getting what he interpreted as a message of encouragement, led his army out to attack Cyrus. But Cyrus defeated him and took the Lydian capital of Sardis in 546 BC.

Cyrus slowly gained control over the whole region and by the time Nabonidus roused himself and returned to Babylon it was too late. A number of his leading generals defected to Cyrus and the city surrendered to him while he was still some miles away so that not a shot was fired and Cyrus himself was welcomed by the citizens of Babylon more as a liberator than a conquerer.

Isaiah of the Exile probably began his ministry before 550 BC when Cyrus was a little known provincial vassal king in the mighty empire of Babylon. God revealed to him his intention of raising this man up and using him as the saviour of Israel to release his people from exile and allow them to go back to the land of Judah and to rebuild Jerusalem. His message at the time must have seemed utterly fantastic. There may be a reference in 41:2 to Cyrus' capture of Ecbatana, his first victory; and 45:1 may possibly refer to his capture of Sardis and his overthrow of the Lydian empire. The next verse 'I will go before you and level the mountains,' is a prophecy of further victories leading up to the overthrow of Babylon itself which is predicted in chapters 46 and 47.

Social and Religious Situation

No one knows the exact number of people who were taken into exile from Judah by the Babylonians. Jerusalem surrendered to Nebuchadnezzar twice. The first time, in the reign of Jehoiachin, was in 597 BC. According to the account in 2 Kings 24: 14 'He carried into exile all Jerusalem; all the officers and fighting men, and all the craftsmen and artisans - a total of ten thousand. Only the poorest people of the land were left.'

The second time Jerusalem surrendered was in the eleventh year of Zedekiah's reign, 587 BC. Zedekiah had been installed by Nebuchadnezzar but had foolishly rebelled against him. This time the Babylonians totally destroyed the city and took the remnant of its citizens into exile. Jeremiah 52:28-30 says that the number totalled 4,600, but this is generally thought to be the men. If we add women and children to that number the total was probably around 12,000 - 15,000. Clearly many people stayed in the land of Judah in farming communities but Jerusalem itself would have been largely deserted.

The difficulty in fixing the precise number taken from Jerusalem into exile is compounded by Jeremiah's statement that in 597 BC only 3,023 were taken away. But the figure of ten thousand in 2 Kings 24 included 7,000 army personnel. It may be that Jeremiah only listed the civilians. Whichever figure we accept, it was a sizeable number who were taken to Babylon. Jeremiah's letter to the first group of exiles (Jeremiah 29:4f) advised them to 'build houses and settle down; plant gardens and eat what they produce. Marry and have sons and daughters.'

There is evidence of regular community life during the Babylonian exile. Ezekiel speaks of elders of the community coming to him (14:1) and seeking his advice which indicates some kind of communal organisation suggesting that they were able to live together and follow their national customs. There are also references in both Ezekiel and Jeremiah to the activity of prophets among the exiles. Jeremiah quoted from a letter (29:24f) sent from Babylon to Jerusalem by Shemaiah who was falsely prophesying among the exiles, and Ezekiel warned against false prophets (13:2f). In his letter, Jeremiah warned the Judeans who had gone into exile in 597 BC that they would be there for a long time but that the Lord had good plans for them and would eventually bring them back. Jeremiah's words appear to have been heeded and regular community life was established.

There is no evidence that the exiles were forced to worship the gods of Babylon and not allowed to practise their own religion. There is, however, plenty of evidence that the exiles were mocked and humiliated. Psalm 137 is a particularly poignant description of the way the masters of Babylon oppressed and humiliated the exiles; *By the rivers of Babylon we sat and wept when we remembered Zion. There on the poplars we hung our harps, for there our captors asked us for songs, our tormentors demanded songs of joy; and they said, "Sing us one of the songs of Zion!"*

The most vivid description of the social and spiritual condition of the exiles is to be found in the book of Lamentations. The 'community laments' found there come from this period and show a dispirited community blaming God for the fall of Jerusalem and for their own wretched condition of slavery. 'You have slain us without pity' they cried out to God. They felt so utterly deserted by the Lord who had abandoned them to their fate and given them into the hands of their enemies that it was no use even engaging in prayer. 'You have covered yourself with a cloud so that no prayer can get through. You have made us scum and refuse among the nations' (Lamentations 3:43-45).

This was the condition of the exiles to whom Isaiah was called to minister. His first task was to raise their confidence in the Lord, to turn their gaze away from their own wretched condition to the greatness and awesome majesty of God. This is why there are so many references in this section to God as the Creator of the universe who holds the nations is his hands and who guides their destiny. This is the God of Israel who has not forgotten his people and is not powerless, but in his own time will bring down even the mighty Babylonian empire and release his people from slavery, sending them back to Zion. Isaiah's ministry was to prepare the way of the Lord who was about to demonstrate his power as the Redeemer of Israel and lead his people back to the land of Judah, to restore the land and spiritually renew the people.

Isaiah the Prophet

W ho was this man to whom God entrusted such an incredible task and gave to him divine revelation that went beyond anything given to earlier prophets? The answer is, quite simply, that no one knows. The difficulty arises from the content and composition of the book of Isaiah. Even reading the book in English it is obvious that there are different sections such as chapters 24 to 27 that are eschatological in character; and chapters 36 to 39 which are historical and are virtually a repeat of the narrative in 2 Kings 18 - 20, and 2 Chronicles 32.

That narrative refers to events in the eighth century when Isaiah of Jerusalem ministered through the reigns of Uzziah to Hezekiah. There are numerous references in chapters 1 to 35 to historical events of that period. Similarly in chapters 40 to 55 there are numerous references to historical events; not to the eighth century, but to two centuries later, the time of Judah's exile in

Babylon. Even the most conservative biblical scholars agree that these chapters all relate to the period of the exile, i.e. from the fall of Jerusalem in 587 BC to the conquest of Babylon by Cyrus the Persian in 539 BC.

The core of the argument among scholars is as to whether God revealed all the details of the exile and the conquest of Babylon by Cyrus some 200 years before it happened. The alternative is that God raised up a prophet during the exile, about 10 or 15 years before the end of the exile, to minister to his fellow countrymen and to prepare them for leaving Babylon.

Conservative scholars take the former view, primarily out of a desire to maintain the single authorship of the book. Liberal scholars take the later view and are primarily concerned with textual and exegetical analyses in positing a multi-authorship. They point out that the vocabulary and style of chapters 1 to 35 is very different from chapters 40 to 55. This, of course, is a powerful argument when put alongside the 200 year difference in contemporary events covered in the prophetic poems.

There is, however, a third way which is taken here and which brings a new dimension to the study of these chapters. It is based upon the revelation of the character of God in scripture and his dealings with the covenant nation of Israel over many centuries of their history. It notes how God has always dealt with his people at the most crucial period of history. From the time of the Judges to Jeremiah, God always raised a man or woman of God for the prophetic task of speaking to the people of that generation. The prophet's mission was to understand the condition of the people and the challenge of the times. Like the tribe of Issachar in David's day the prophets had to be those 'who understood the times and knew what Israel should do' (1 Chronicles 12:32).

In chapters 40 - 55 we see the passionate outpouring of a man of immense spiritual stature who has fully identified with the plight of his people. He clearly knows what it is like to feel abandoned and comfortless. He knows this because he is one of 'a people plundered and looted, all of them trapped in pits or hidden away in prisons. They have become plunder, with no one to rescue them; they have been made loot with no one to say, "Send them back"' (42:22). He had also seen the elaborate idolatry of

Babylon and watched the craftsmen at work fashioning wooden images for pagan worshipers (44:9-20) and he had learned that none of these gods was able to answer the petitions of their devotees.

Isaiah of the Exile was not only a keen observer of the contemporary scene, he was also one who was called and anointed by God. He had heard the voice of the living God saying 'Cry out!' and he had responded 'What shall I cry?' (40:6). From that moment he began receiving divine revelation on a plane not previously ascended by any of the prophets.

He was shown that there is only one God, creator of all things, who is none other than the covenant God of Israel, who, because he was sovereign Lord of the nations, was able to use a pagan king to redeem his people from slavery and send them back to Judah. Isaiah's words of praise show that he was overwhelmed with the magnitude of this message and his own compassion and joy overflowed as he identified with the word given to him by the Lord.

'Comfort, comfort my people,' was a message that he himself had first received and then passed on to his fellow countrymen. Together they had paid a high price for the sins of their fathers. But now their hard service was completed and they had indeed 'received from the Lord's hand double' for their sins (40:2). Isaiah called on the heavens and the earth to rejoice and 'burst into song ... for the Lord comforts his people and will have compassion on his afflicted ones' (49:13).

Isaiah's mission was to transform a demoralised, faithless, hopeless, status-less community, lacking in any sense of self-worth or any confidence in the God of their fathers, into people of vibrant faith awaiting the day when their God would overthrow the most powerful empire in the world on behalf of them, his chosen people. Their trust in the Lord had to be built up to such a point where they were willing to face the rigours and hardships of the long trek back to Zion.

This was the mission God entrusted to Isaiah of the Exile. Such a task could only have been carried out by a man who was fully identified with his people and totally committed to the Lord and filled with the Spirit of God. It was not a mission that could have been achieved through a scroll written 200 years earlier that had somehow survived the destruction of Jerusalem and the Temple and had somehow reached Babylon to be read to the exiles by one of their elders. The message had to be embodied in a man actually experiencing the events of the times along with his people; 'Come near to me and listen to this' he said to the people, for this is the word of the living God, who has 'tested you in the furnace of affliction' (48:10) but whose 'unfailing love for you will not be shaken' (54:10), 'from the first announcement I have not spoken in secret; *at the time it happens*, I am there' (48:16).

These messages were living messages from a living God freshly imparted into the contemporary scene. If further proof were needed that what we have here in chapters 40 to 55 is the ministry of a prophet who was living among the people and fully immersed in the scene of his labours, it is to be found in the reaction of the people to the message and the prophet's response. They scorned the pronouncement that God would use Cyrus the foreign king as a 'Shepherd' and a 'Redeemer' of Israel. Isaiah had to explain that God could do this because he held the nations in his hands 'as a drop in a bucket'; ALL the nations, not just Israel! This was the new teaching which went far beyond anything taught by the eighth century prophets including Isaiah of Jerusalem and even went beyond the teaching of Jeremiah earlier in the sixth century.

The prophet makes no attempt to identify himself although some scholars think that 40:6-8 represents the call and commissioning of the prophet which some commentators see as a parallel to the account of Isaiah of Jerusalem's encounter with the Lord in Isaiah 6. The only other possible reference to the personal identity of the prophet is to be found in 49:1f, in the statement 'Before I was born the Lord called me; from my birth he has made mention of my name.' This, however, may be a poetic reference to the servanthood of the nation, hence 'He said to me, "You are my servant, Israel, in whom I will display my splendour"' (49:3).The identity of the prophet was not a problem in ancient Israel as it is for us in the modern western world. We are obsessed with inquisitiveness to know every detail of the lives of our modern heroes and pop idols. We want to know where they live and how they live, what clothes they wear, what food they eat and what they do in the privacy of their own homes.

This was not the culture in ancient Israel. Among those who preserved the words of the great prophets of Israel the only thing that really mattered was the preservation of words which they believed came from God himself. The prophets were regarded as the mouthpiece of the Lord, therefore the messenger was unimportant once the authenticity of his words had been established. The focus was upon the Lord, not on a man.

We know that there was a little school of prophets in Jerusalem who looked to Jeremiah as their leader and who after his death faithfully preserved his words. In the same way there was an Isaianic school of prophecy a hundred and twenty years earlier than Jeremiah, who also faithfully preserved the words of their master. How the words of Isaiah of the Exile came to be attached to those of Isaiah of Jerusalem who lived 200 years earlier is quite unknown. What is more, does it really matter? Surely what matters is that we have here in this middle section of the book of Isaiah some of the most precious words of the whole Bible.

It really is a fruitless exercise to try to prove that Isaiah of Jerusalem, 200 years earlier, knew every detail of the exile and the history of that period simply in order to try to preserve the unity of the book of Isaiah. To do so is to misunderstand the nature and purpose of prophecy. God always raised up prophets in times of crisis or special need in the history of his covenant people. They were men of their times whose special task was to understand the times and to bring the contemporary word of the contemporary God to the contemporary scene.

Of course God could have revealed all these things to one of his servants 200 years earlier but why would he do that? Why would he not do as he always did in raising up a prophet among the exiles to speak to his own people as the mouthpiece of God? Those who believe in the unity of the book of Isaiah are free to do so and they will find nothing offensive in these studies but I would not be true to my own understanding of the ministry of the prophet if I did not state my own beliefs. For me, it is not important to know the identity of the man behind the message, my only concern is with the message itself and with seeking to understand the word of the living God so powerfully conveyed through these chapters. Furthermore I do not believe it is possible to understand the message without seeing it in the context of the exile in Babylon and God ministering to his people in those circumstances. I am perfectly happy to call the prophet 'Isaiah' as with his illustrious eighth century predecessor of the same name. After all, it was a pretty common name, as it is today in modern Israel.

The Message

Like all the great prophets of Israel Isaiah completely identified with his people. His great compassion and love for his fellow countrymen are clearly conveyed from the very first words of chapter 40, 'Comfort, comfort my people, says your God. Speak tenderly to Jerusalem, and proclaim to her that her hard service has been completed, that her sin has been paid for.' He was fully aware of the community laments as portrayed in the book of Lamentations and the complaints of the people against the Lord. 'The Lord is like an enemy; he has swallowed up Israel' (Lamentations 2:5). Isaiah's task was to bring a message of redemption and salvation, but his starting point was to identify with the people and to begin where they were. Without that identification the message could never have been heard. The people had sunk so deeply into self-pity and the loss of any sense of self-worth that a trite message of hope and good cheer would not have been heard. It would have been rejected out of hand.

Isaiah began where the people were, recognising their terrible suffering and abject humiliation. His task then was to build up their faith and confidence in the Lord so that they were ready actively to play their part in God's purpose of restoration for Israel and rebuilding the life of the nation. In order to communicate the message that he had been given, God entrusted him with a degree of self-revelation that none of the prophets had received since the time of Moses. There is a sense in which each of the prophets received a unique part of the revelation of God but Isaiah was taken to greater spiritual depths than any of his predecessors.

The revelation that Isaiah of the Exile was given was a great leap forward in understanding the very nature of God. He was not only pre-eminent among the gods, he was the only God. He was not only active in the history of the nation in the past, but he was preparing to do something greater than he had ever previously performed in any generation of Israel's history. This act of deliverance of the exiles from Babylon would even put the exodus from Egypt into the shade. But Isaiah was seeing beyond the mere physical restoration of the people to the land to the true significance of the spiritual restoration of the people. This was what the covenant relationship with God was all about.

Israel had never understood the purpose of that covenant. Usually it had been seen in terms of its benefits to the nation rather than in terms of servanthood. Isaiah was shown that the true destiny of Israel as the servant of the Lord was to be a light for the Gentiles. It was God's intention to use his covenant people as the means through whom he would reveal himself to the whole world, to the unbelieving nations of the Gentiles.

In order to prepare the way for a message of this magnitude God had to establish it in the minds of his people. They had to learn that God was not only the one and only God but that he was also the actual Creator of the entire universe. He spread the stars in the sky; they were the work of his hands. It was this same God who was the almighty, all powerful, Lord of the universe who actually had taken little Israel, the family of Jacob, and blessed them and watched over them and built them up into a great nation so that they could be his true servant in the world.

The message of salvation included many reassurances that God had not forgotten his people, that even though he had allowed them to go into exile because of their sinfulness and faithlessness he had never forgotten them. Indeed God had etched their name upon his hands, because he loved them with an unending love. 'Can a mother forget the baby at her breast and have no compassion on the child she has born?' he asked. Although Israel's faithlessness had broken her covenant relationship with God, God himself had never forsaken his covenant people. In due time he would restore them to the land he had promised to their forefathers.

The time of deliverance was rapidly drawing near but God was about to use a foreign king to accomplish his purposes. He was well able to do this because he was the Lord of history who held the destiny of the nations in his hands. But the whole purpose of God's act of salvation of his people and returning them to the land was to carry out the spiritual restoration of the people so that they could be the instrument in his hands to reveal his nature and purposes to the whole world. This task is foreseen in the Servant Songs which are the climax of this section of the book of Isaiah. They represent the idealised Israel in the person of the Servant. As such they personify the salvation that God intends to bring to all peoples throughout the world through the Servant.

Isaiah of Jerusalem had foreseen that due to the sinfulness of the nation the purposes of God could not be fulfilled through the whole nation collectively. He foresaw that God would use a righteous remnant to carry out his purposes. This righteous remnant is now foreseen in this section of the book of Isaiah as being the cleansed, redeemed and restored people of the exile who return to Zion with great rejoicing and filled with praise and trust in the Lord. Even so, Isaiah of the Exile foresaw that this righteous remnant could not fully carry out the purposes of God but that God would eventually raise up a righteous one in the person of the Servant, his Messiah who through redemptive suffering would bring salvation to all mankind.

This is the climax of the message 'we all, like sheep, have gone astray, each of us has turned to his own way; and the Lord has laid on him the iniquity of us all'. Isaiah was given the message that paved the way for the great gospel declaration that 'God so loved the world that he gave his one and only Son, that whoever believes in him shall not perish but have eternal life. For God did not send his Son into the world to condemn the world, but to save the world through him' (John 3:16-17).

These studies in Isaiah 40-53 prepare the way for a greater understanding of those verses in John's Gospel that are at the heart of God's plan of salvation for all people.

Clifford Hill

THE COMFORT OF GOD

Isaiah 40: 1-2

Comfort, comfort my people, says your God. Speak tenderly to Jerusalem, and proclaim to her that her hard service has been completed, that her sin has been paid for, that she has received from the Lord's hand double for all her sins.

Comment

This beautiful message exemplifies the love of God for his people. Their plight had been seen; their cries had been heard; their suffering had aroused the compassion of their God. From the heart of cruel Babylon, centre of world oppression, this message of hope was sent to the once great city of Jerusalem whose people toiled in slavery.

'Comfort, comfort my people, says your God. Speak tenderly to Jerusalem'. How strange it must have seemed to the remnant of Judah, still living in and around the ruins of Jerusalem, to receive such a message. In times past the great prophets of Israel had thundered out messages to Babylon from Jerusalem. But this was the first time that process had been reversed. Clearly something of great significance was happening; a new age was dawning.

The prophetic voice of hope, however, was not only directed to Jerusalem but the message was primarily intended for the exiles in Babylon. The years of servitude had broken their spirit. Hopelessness and despair had overwhelmed them. They were not only physically separated from Jerusalem by many hundreds of miles, but with the destruction of the temple, seen by their captors as the triumph of the gods of Babylon, the God of Israel appeared powerless and defeated.

The vivid description in Psalm 137 of the people sitting weeping by the rivers of Babylon when they remembered all that had happened to Jerusalem, gives a little of the background to this momentous message. Its significance is underlined by the repetition of the word 'comfort'.

Such repetition is often used for emphasis in this section of Isaiah, such as 'awake, awake' (51:9) and 'Awake, Awake!' (51:17), literally this wake up call means, 'Arouse yourself, arouse yourself' (51:17). It is a call to shake out of the stupor of sleepiness that had overtaken the nation. The terrible experience of the destruction of Jerusalem and the years of oppression had taken their toll.

This message of comfort is the opening announcement that climaxes in the exhortation to leave Babylon. Once again the impact of the message is increased by repetition, 'Depart, depart!' (52:11). Thus the word 'comfort' is not to be interpreted as a mere cosy hug! God was not simply commiserating with his people in their suffering. This was a prophetic call to action with the announcement that God was about to do something dramatic to relieve the suffering of his people.

The word 'comfort' here implies a positive action of restoration; a promise of God's intervention to change the circumstances of his people. Their time of servitude was ended. They had suffered for their sins and the sins of their forefathers. Now was the time of release. God himself had paid the price of redemption and now his people would be free to leave the place of captivity.

This is a message to all those who find themselves in difficult circumstances, whether of their own making or not. When we cry out to the Lord for help our cries are never ignored. The Lord simply waits for the right moment to intervene to bring help and comfort to his children.

Prayer
Lord, we bless you that you do hear our prayers for help in our times of weakness and despair. Thank you for this message of comfort.

PREPARE THE WAY

Isaiah 40: 3- 5

A voice of one calling: "In the desert prepare the way for the Lord; make straight in the wilderness a highway for our God. Every valley shall be raised up, every mountain and hill made low; the rough ground shall become level, the rugged places a plain. And the glory of the Lord will be revealed, and all mankind together will see it. For the mouth of the Lord has spoken."

Comment

This is a key passage setting out the theme for the whole of the second half of the book of Isaiah. There is no identification of the messenger; the announcement simply refers to a 'voice' calling out a prophetic message. It is the declaration that God is about to visit the land, and it is a call to be prepared to see the coming of the Lord.

It is unclear from the text whether the reference to the desert is part of the message (as in the NIV) or whether it is the location of the messenger (as in the AV), 'The voice of him that crieth in the wilderness'. The AV rendering of the next line is much to be preferred - 'Prepare the way of the Lord' rather than 'Prepare the way for the Lord'. The Hebrew text could be translated either way, but it is surely sheer human arrogance that thinks we can prepare the way for the Lord - to do something for him that he himself cannot do. Our responsibility is to be ready when God comes to us, prepared to receive him.

Scholars are divided on the interpretation of this passage. Some think it refers to the release of the captives from Babylon and their journey home, seeing it as a demonstration of the power of God. Kings often returned home in triumph after battle with a victory parade and it is possible that what the prophet is foreseeing is the overthrow of Babylon as an act of God. This will result in his glory being seen by 'all mankind' in the return of the exiles to Jerusalem.

Other scholars see this as a divine visitation, of God coming from Mount Sinai and clearing the way ahead of him in preparation for a mighty act in the land of Israel that will demonstrate his power and glory to all the world. The fact that all people will see it makes it an extraordinary event which suggests it refers to the coming of Messiah. There is great certainty in the message because 'the mouth of the Lord has spoken' therefore it will happen. The glorious presence of God will one day be revealed to the whole world.

Paul sounds the same note of absolute conviction when he declares that the day will come when 'at the name of Jesus every knee should bow, in heaven and on earth and under the earth, and every tongue confess that Jesus Christ is Lord, to the glory of God the Father' (Philippians 2:10-11).

In the darkest days, when our faith is being severely tested by difficult circumstances, we can turn to this absolute certainty that God will fulfil his purposes. He himself has declared it. The day will surely come when all the nations will see the glory of God and he will reveal himself to all people. As believers in the Lord Jesus there is a place reserved for each one of us in his glorious Kingdom.

Prayer
Thank you, Lord, that your victory is sure and certain and that we have a place in your family.

THE WORD OF GOD

Isaiah 40: 6- 8
A voice says, "Cry out." And I said, "What shall I cry?"
"All men are like grass, and all their glory is like the flowers
of the field. The grass withers and the flowers fall, because
the breath of the Lord blows on them. Surely the people are
grass. The grass withers and the flowers fall, but the word
of our God stands forever."

Comment

This passage contrasts with the previous one where 'a voice' calls out and gives a message. Here the voice issues a command to 'cry out!' The prophet responds, 'What shall I cry?' The message given to the prophet to proclaim could hardly be of greater contrast to the previous passage which depicted God moving in triumph across the land, raising valleys and flattening mountains. Now the scene moves from God to humanity, from power to powerlessness, from divine glory to frail flesh.

The two contrasting pictures are a deliberate attempt to show that humanity's only hope is in God. There is nothing more frail than grass. It grows quickly but, subjected to drought and scorching heat, it withers in a couple of days. The wild flowers that grow among the grass are equally frail. They too wither and fall when conditions are not favourable.

The prophet probably had in mind the hot, dry, sandstorm type of winds that occasionally blow from the desert and quickly destroy vegetation, turning everything from green to brown, withering and decaying the harvest that once looked so promising.

Jesus used the frailty of grass to illustrate his teaching on the impermanency of material things. But he also appreciated the beauty of a field of grass laced with wild flowers. He compared it to the splendour of Solomon. But the real point that Jesus was illustrating was that God really cares for his people. He said, 'If that is how God clothes the grass of the field, which is here today and tomorrow is thrown into the fire, will he not much more clothe you, O you of little faith?' (Matthew 6:30).

Similarly the reason for these verses in Isaiah 40 is not to depress the people but to remind them of the power of God and his absolute dependability. The announcement of God's salvation in verses 3-5, foretelling a mighty divine intervention to rescue the people from the grip of the enemy, may have fallen upon incredulous ears. 'How can this be true?' the people were asking.

The mighty Babylonian Empire appeared impregnable, so here God reminds his people that all humanity is as frail as grass. This paves the way for the great pronouncements in chapters 45-47 of the impending fall of Babylon. The reason that Babylon cannot stand and will be just like the grass of the field is that God has determined to bring about her downfall and 'the word of our God stands for ever'.

That is the real message of this passage, that nothing can stand against the word of God. What he determines to do, he will accomplish. His word stands for ever. It is a message we need to hear every day because it is so easy to get distracted by the pressures of life so that we overlook the power of God.

We become so immersed in our daily work, or in household chores, or family responsibilities, that we have little time or strength to meditate, or to sit quietly in the presence of the Lord. We are frail, just like the grass. But God knows our frailty and the pressures upon us. He wants to remind us that he loves us and wants us to trust him completely to work out his good purposes, for 'the word of our God stands for ever'.

Prayer

Lord, help me to take my eyes off the world and to focus upon your word that stands for ever.

GOOD TIDINGS

Isaiah 40: 9- 11

**You who bring good tidings to Zion, go up on a high
mountain. You who bring good tidings to Jerusalem, lift up
your voice with a shout, lift it up, do not be afraid; say to the
towns of Judah, "Here is your God!" See, the Sovereign
Lord comes with power and his arm rules for him. See, his
reward is with him, and his recompense accompanies him.
He tends his flock like a shepherd: He gathers the lambs in
his arms and carries them close to his heart; he gently leads
those that have young.**

Comment

The previous three passages have all been to prepare the way
for the main message. They were the 'starters', the *'hors-
d'oeuvres'*, to prepare the palate of the eater for the main meal.
The prophet now brings the central message. He moves into his
main theme with great urgency and enthusiasm. The Lord is
coming!

That is the good news. It is not a philosophical concept, or a
theological proposition. It is a simple fact showing the way God
works. When he wants to accomplish the salvation of his people,
to rescue them from the grip of the enemy, he does not send them
a set of rules like a book of instructions accompanying a DIY kit
for self-assembly. He himself comes to his people.

God had already sent his Torah - the teaching given to Moses -
and he had established his covenant with his people. But the
teaching had been neglected and the covenant broken and
disaster had followed disaster. Now God himself was coming to
break the power of the enemy and to bring release to his people.

The messenger was instructed to go up on a high mountain
and to shout aloud the good tidings. Just as the watchman, high
up on the watchtower, used to shout the message or blow the
shofah which could be heard all over the city, so Zion, which in

this case stands for the whole people of Israel, was to proclaim a message to all the villages and towns across the land. The NIV translation misses the most important point here by saying that the messenger was to bring good tidings TO Jerusalem and TO Zion. The AV and the NIV margin both recognise that it is *Jerusalem* that is the one who is to declare the good news of God, 'O Zion, bringer of good tidings, go up onto a high mountain, O Jerusalem, bringer of good tidings.' This catches the real essence of the passage in which God is calling upon the people of Jerusalem and the people of Israel to be a prophetic people. They are to declare the coming of the Lord to all the towns and cities of the land so that it goes out far and wide across the world.

They are told not to be afraid to declare the message NOW, even though it has not yet happened. God IS coming. His word is unbreakable. He will bring the exiles back from captivity. But the good news is that he himself is coming and bringing the people with him just like a conquering king comes bringing the booty of war with him. But Zion's Saviour comes with tenderness, his glory is not the swaggering of a warrior king. He carries the weak in his arms as a shepherd carries the lambs that cannot keep up with the flock. He gently leads the sick, the lame and the elderly.

This message is still relevant today. God wants his people to be a prophetic people, telling the world about his good purposes and being unafraid to say that he is coming again, SOON! The first time he came was to bring salvation, but the next time he comes will be to judge the nations.

Prayer
Lord, stir up your people to declare your message to the world. Make us unafraid to speak your word to those around us.

THE LORD OF CREATION

Isaiah 40: 12- 14

Who has measured the waters in the hollow of his hand, or with the breadth of his hand marked off the heavens? Who has held the dust of the earth in a basket, or weighed the mountains on the scales and the hills in a balance? Who has understood the mind of the Lord, or instructed him as his counsellor? Whom did the Lord consult to enlighten him, and who taught him the right way? Who was it that taught him knowledge or showed him the path of understanding?

Comment

This passage contains a number of rhetorical questions that demand an answer from the hearer or reader. The questions are, 'Who has measured?' 'Who has weighed?' 'Who has comprehended?' and 'Who has taught?'

The questions are framed to demonstrate the uniqueness of God. This may seem unnecessary to modern minds brought up in a monotheistic culture. But in Isaiah's day the surrounding nations all recognised a pantheon of gods. To declare that there was only one God who created the universe, the stars in the heavens, as well as the world, the land and the sea, was a daring departure from conventional wisdom. To declare further that this God of creation was not only the one and only God, but he was also personal, one who could be communicated with, was unheard of.

This was the message for which this opening section of the second half of the book of Isaiah is designed to prepare the way. Hence the questions here are part of the theme that will unfold in the later chapters. The prophet was bringing a revolutionary message radically different from anything in the contemporary pagan religions and different from anything previously heard in Israel.

Who has measured the waters on earth or the distances between the galaxies in the heavens, or weighed the mountains and hills? The questions demand the answer - only God! The next questions (vv13 and 14) require a different answer. 'Who has comprehended the Spirit of the Lord?' (this is a better translation than the NIV, 'Who has understood the mind of the Lord?') This is not referring to the Holy Spirit, the third person of the Trinity, but to the whole being of God. This is in line with the teaching of Jesus, 'God is spirit and those who worship him must worship in spirit and in truth' (John 4:24). The answer is 'No-one!' No-one can fully comprehend God. Who has instructed God? Who has taught him? Who has shown him the way of justice and righteousness? Again the answer is, 'No-one!'

God is unique. He is the Lord of creation. There is none like him. That is the prophet's opening declaration. This prepares the ground for the revelation of God's purposes and the great act of salvation he intends accomplishing for all mankind. This was the unique message of hope for all mankind for which these opening verses of chapter 40 were intended to prepare the way.

One of the things our modern world lacks is a sense of awe. The political correctness of western democracy has elevated 'equality' above 'respect' or any other consideration. Even modern Christian worship has substituted a matey relationship with God, 'Abba', 'Daddy' for the awesome reality of the Lord of creation. This is a timely reminder of the immense power of the Almighty God, who has chosen to reveal himself through the prophets and apostles, and uniquely in his Son - Yeshua Ha'Mashiach.

Prayer

Lord, we do thank you that through Jesus we are able to know you as 'Our Father'. Help us never to forget that you are also the Lord of creation who sustains the universe by your immeasurable power.

THE INCOMPARABLE GOD

Isaiah 40: 15- 19

Surely the nations are like a drop in a bucket; they are regarded as dust on the scales; he weighs the islands as though they were fine dust. Lebanon is not sufficient for altar fires, nor its animals enough for burnt offerings. Before him all the nations are as nothing; they are regarded by him as worthless and less than nothing. To whom, then, will you compare God? What image will you compare him to? As for an idol, a craftsman casts it, and a goldsmith overlays it with gold and fashions silver chains for it.

Comment

The imagery here is of a woman filling her bucket at the well and although the water that she carries is precious, she doesn't bother with the odd drop that drips from the bottom of the bucket as she lifts it out of the well. One drop is of no consequence. Similarly, when the corn is weighed on the scales and poured into a container for the housewife at the market, there is always some dust left on the scales. But that doesn't trouble her. It is of no account, worthless in comparison to the full measure of corn.

In the same way, the God of Israel regards the other nations, including the great empires of man such as Assyria and Babylon. They are of no more value than a drop that falls from the bottom of the bucket or the fine dust left on the scales in the market.

The God of Israel, who is the Lord of creation, is so great that if the nations were to try to worship him, even all the beautiful wood from the cedar forests of Lebanon would not be adequate for an altar fire, neither would there be sufficient animals for sacrifice. In fact, before the majesty of the one true God, the nations of the world are as nothing, in fact, less than nothing!

Therefore, if whole nations of men and women are as nothing before God, how much more insignificant are wooden idols!

Even if men select wood that will not rot (v20) and goldsmiths overlay it with precious metals, it is still only a lifeless idol with no power. The key statement here is, 'To whom, then, will you compare God?' He is incomparable. He has no equal. He is the Almighty One, the Creator of the ends of the universe. He stretched out the heavens, he divided the land from the sea and set the nations in their places.

All this is to say to Israel, the people through whom God had chosen to reveal himself to the world, that they had nothing to fear from men! It is the same message that all the prophets, from the eighth century onwards declared, that the people of God should not put their trust in the empires of man, but neither should they be afraid of them.

This is a message that is still relevant today. As the people of God we have nothing to fear from those who are hostile to the gospel. They are only human. We have still less to fear from the great institutions of men that are their modern gods, whom the world idolises and worships. They are all part of modern Babylon which God regards as a mere drop in a bucket. As Jesus said to his followers, 'Fear not little flock, for it is your Father's good pleasure to give you the kingdom' (Luke 12:32 AV).

Let all the people know that our God is more powerful than all the massed armies of the unbelieving nations. His purposes will be fulfilled, for his word stands for ever. If at any time you are under attack from unbelievers let this be your comfort and your strength.

Prayer
Lord, there is no offering of praise and worship that we can bring to you that is worthy of your greatness, goodness and love. May the service of our lives be an offering acceptable in your sight today.

GOD OF THE UNIVERSE

Isaiah 40: 21- 24

Do you not know? Have you not heard? Has it not been
told you from the beginning? Have you not understood
since the earth was founded? He sits enthroned above the
circle of the earth, and its people are like grasshoppers. He
stretches out the heavens like a canopy, and spreads them
out like a tent to live in. He brings princes to naught and
reduces the rulers of this world to nothing. No sooner are
they planted, no sooner are they sown, no sooner do they
take root in the ground, than he blows on them and they
wither, and a whirlwind sweeps them away like chaff.

Comment

Continuing the theme of the one true God, Creator of all
things, the prophet expresses amazement that Israel, the
people who have for generations had a special revelation of him
through the prophets, has not understood their God. 'Do you not
know? Have you not heard?' he asks. Surely from the time of the
patriarchs it should have been clear to all Israel that the God who
revealed his Torah to Moses, and has spoken through the
prophets, is the only power in the universe. 'He sits enthroned
above the circle of the earth'.

This is an amazing statement. Was it revealed to Isaiah
hundreds of years before Galileo, the fifteenth century
astronomer, that the earth was not flat? (Or was it Ptolemy, the
second century Greek mathematician, who was the first to
discover that the earth was round?) What did Isaiah mean by 'the
circle of the earth'? The Egyptians had been studying astronomy
for at least 2500 years before Isaiah and using their knowledge to
predict the periods when the Nile would flood. They knew that
the heavenly bodies, including the sun and the moon, moved in
circular fashion. But they thought of the earth as the centre of the
universe around which all the solar system revolved.

Isaiah may simply here be using conventional wisdom to express the revelation he had received of God being at the centre of the universe. He created every star and the sun and the moon, stretching out the heavens like a gigantic tent for people to live in. The people themselves appeared like grasshoppers to God. Even the rulers of the nations are nothing in comparison with the almighty power of God. Worldly empires founded by man, however powerful and impregnable they may seem, have no permanence. 'No sooner are they planted' and God blows upon them and they are destroyed.

The relevance for Israel was that God had already said to Jeremiah that Babylon, the mighty empire that dominated the world, would only last 70 years. Isaiah was preparing the ground for the announcement that time was up for Babylon. God was about to overthrow it and release his people. Babylon had run its course. The proud empire that had terrorised the middle east for two generations was about to disappear.

A modern analogy is the rise and fall of the Communist empire of the Soviet Union in the twentieth century. Once again God allowed 70 years for a mighty empire of man that declared 'there is no God'. Once again God looked upon the grasshoppers that set up that atheistic empire to dominate the world. It was just 70 years from the 1916 Bolshevik revolution to the meltdown of the Chernobyl nuclear reactor in 1986 that began the meltdown of the USSR. Our God is never in a hurry, but he always fulfils his word. We should never be dismayed by the evil powers arranged against us, but rather look to the Lord who holds the nations in his hands and who will eventually destroy them.

Prayer
Lord, help us never to be dismayed when the powers of evil appear to be triumphing and darkness is all around. Strengthen your people with your great power and love that we may stand firm even in difficult days.

THE EVERLASTING GOD

Isaiah 40: 25- 27
**"To whom will you compare me? Or who is my equal?"
says the Holy One. Lift your eyes and look to the heavens:
Who created all these? He who brings out the starry host
one by one, and calls them each by name. Because of his
great power and mighty strength, not one of them is
missing. Why do you say, O Jacob, and complain, O Israel,
"My way is hidden from the Lord; my cause is disregarded
by my God"?**

Comment

Once again the challenge to compare is issued. In v18 it was
the prophet who asked the question. Now it is God himself
who asks, 'To whom will you compare me? Or who is my equal?'
The questioner is named as 'Holy One'.

Interestingly, there is no article in the Hebrew, indicating that
this was a personal name. He was 'Holy One' the God of Israel,
the one who was separated from the whole of creation. He was
the 'Wholly Other', the Lord of creation, who had set each of the
stars in their courses. He challenges those who question his
power to look up into the night sky and gaze at the starry host.
He put each of them there and he calls each one of them by
name.

The contrast here is with the Canaanite belief in many gods
who were linked with these heavenly bodies. But the God of
Israel is the one who brought them into being and gave them
each their name.

Again, this is a deliberate comparison because conventional
wisdom said that if you knew someone's name it gave you
power over them. Hence Jesus was said to know the demons by
name so he had power to cast them out. Here, God is shown as
the one whose power and mighty strength sustains the universe
and ensures that none of the millions of stars that light up the sky
on the clear night are missing.

Halfway through this passage we come to the real purpose of the whole chapter. Having extravagantly set the scene, emphasising the almighty power of Israel's God, Creator of all things, he now demands, 'Why do you say, O Jacob, and complain, O Israel, "My way is hidden from the Lord, my cause is hidden from my God?"'

The whole context is clearly intended to show the absurdity of Israel's complaint that God neither sees nor hears the cries of his people in slavery in Babylon. Their just cause is not hidden from him. How could it be hidden from the One who controls the whole universe and who creates and destroys stars in the sky and the passing empires of man? It is utterly impossible for such a God to overlook the plight of his own people, for he is not like the dumb wooden idols of the pagans. He is the living God who is almighty and all powerful.

It is all too easy to think that God has forgotten us when daily pleas for help appear to go unanswered. We often forget that God's timing is not our timing and that no prayer ever goes unanswered. Sometimes God's answer has to be, 'No, that is not the best for you'. Or, 'Wait, the time is not yet right'. In times of darkness God says, 'Now look up into the night sky and see the heavenly host. Who created these? Who keeps them in their course? It is I, the everlasting God, and I love you my child. I have not forgotten you. I will ensure that all things work together for your good.'

Sometimes it is good to go for a walk on a clear night when the sky is lit with millions of stars. It reminds us of the greatness of our God and our own smallness. But it should also fill us with wonder that the God of all creation actually cares for each one of us his children – the ones for whom Jesus died.

Prayer

Lord, I love you. Help me to trust you more and more each day.

STRENGTH TO THE WEARY

Isaiah 40: 28- 31

Do you not know? Have you not heard? The Lord is the everlasting God, the Creator of the ends of the earth. He will not grow tired or weary, and his understanding no one can fathom. He gives strength to the weary and increases the power of the weak. Even youths grow tired and weary, and young men stumble and fall; but those who hope in the Lord will renew their strength. They will soar on wings like eagles; they will run and not grow weary, they will walk and not be faint.

Comment

We come now to the climax of chapter 40 and in it is set out the theme for the rest of the book of Isaiah. God, 'the everlasting God, Creator of the ends of the earth', never grows weary and no-one can fully understand his purposes. But he is the almighty God, King of the universe, and he will never desert his covenant people. He is about to intervene in the course of human history, to overthrow mighty empires and raise up others who will fulfil his purpose. This was the message that was revealed to the prophet.

The scene was now set for the announcement which the captives had longed to hear as they sat and wept beside the rivers of Babylon listening to their tormentors demanding that they sing songs of Zion. 'How can we sing songs of the Lord while in a foreign land?' (Psalm 137). Soon they would no longer be slaves; the voices of their tormentors would be silenced, their gods defeated and overthrown. Soon they would be singing 'the songs of ascent' (Psalms 120 - 134) as they climbed up the long trail to reach Mount Zion, as pilgrims seeking their God. He could foresee the long trail of returning refugees, a bedraggled, footsore company of all ages. The elderly, families with young children, the strong and the weak, would all set out with high hopes and great enthusiasm. But the long journey would take its toll of their strength. They were going to need more than mere human endeavour if they were to reach Zion in safety.

Having set the scene and prepared the ground for the message that would lift the hearts of the exiles, the prophet was foreseeing the testing times ahead as the released exiles made the long and arduous journey home. In a vision, he saw the strength draining from the weary travellers as they walked mile after mile along rough roads and difficult terrain. He saw that the most essential thing they needed before the time came for them to leave Babylon, was trust in God. The whole of chapter 40 carries the message of God's almighty power in which the people could have absolute confidence. Now he spelt out in practical terms the lessons the exiles most needed to learn before the day of their release. The journey would be such that even young men would grow weary, but those who had learned to trust the Lord in the darkest hours of exile would be sustained. They were the ones whose hope was in the Lord and they would renew their strength. In fact, they would soar like eagles, 'Run and not grow weary ... Walk and not faint'.

Often at the beginning of a new job, or on taking up new responsibilities, we soar on wings like eagles, being carried by enthusiasm. But as excitement dies and novelty turns to routine, the adrenalin drains away. It is then that we have to rely on the strength of the Lord. But that is what he wants from the beginning. He assures us that if our hope is in him, even if we can no longer run and we slow down to a walk, he will make sure that we do not faint. He renews our strength every morning and carries us through the day.

Prayer

Lord, you are the only one who can sustain your people through every circumstance of life. My hope is in you, my strength and my Redeemer.

ALPHA AND OMEGA

Isaiah 41: 1- 4

"Be silent before me, you islands! Let the nations renew
their strength! Let them come forward and speak; let us
meet together at the place of judgment. Who has stirred up
one from the east, calling him in righteousness to his
service? He hands nations over to him and subdues kings
before him. He turns them to dust with his sword, to wind-
blown chaff with his bow. He pursues them and moves on
unscathed, by a path his feet have not travelled before. Who
has done this and carried it through, calling forth the
generations from the beginning? I, the Lord – with the first
of them and with the last – I am he."

Comment

This is a courtroom scene. The prophet sees the Lord God,
whom he has identified as the Lord of Creation, the Ruler of
the universe, calling the nations to a place of judgment. The call
goes out to all nations. 'The islands' signifies the ends of the
earth. It may be that the British Isles is referred to here as the
farthest known point off the west coast of Europe.

All nations are summoned to stand in silence while the charge
is read out. At issue is the fact that all the nations have gods for
whom they claim divinity. But God has revealed to the prophets
of Israel that there is only one God. So who is the true God? That
is the subject on trial.

The first evidence brought by the Lord is that he has called
into his service 'one from the east'. Although this person is not
named it is perfectly obvious that it is Cyrus, the Persian king.
His identity may not have been so clear at that time since the
Babylonian Empire was still at its height and appeared
impregnable.

The main point of God's claim to divinity is that he is
different from the gods of the other nations. Here that claim is

based upon his ability to foretell future events that were destined to change the course of history. Cyrus was going to find his conquests made easy by the God of Israel going before him and handing over nations to him. He would pursue them so quickly that his feet would hardly touch the ground.

The final submission in this courtroom drama is when God calls the nations to witness that he is the One who has existed since the beginning of creation and he will be there to the last. His name is I AM - the Alpha and Omega. He is not only pre-existent to all history, but he holds all things under his control. He is the one who has called into being one generation after another, because he is the giver of life. The Lord's own testimony is that he was there with the first generation and he will be there with the last. He is the Lord of history who holds the nations and their destiny in his hands.

It is surely a comfort to know that God still holds the destiny of nations in his hands, especially in dark periods of world events when there seems no end to the violence of war or to the wickedness of human beings. The rapid changes in the world since the middle of the twentieth century created an unstable environment for the twenty-first century with a poor outlook for world peace.

But God does work out his purposes despite the wickedness of the nations. Moreover, he watches over those who love him and ensures their protection and their good despite even the heaviest blows of the enemy. He not only creates life, but he remains with his beloved ones to the end of time, not only in this life but into all eternity.

Prayer

Lord Jesus, thank you that you have promised to abide with us and that you will be with us for ever, even to the end of time.

I WILL UPHOLD YOU!

Isaiah 41: 8- 11

"But you, O Israel, my servant, Jacob, whom I have chosen, you descendants of Abraham my friend, I took you from the ends of the earth, from its farthest corners I called you. I said, 'You are my servant'; I have chosen you and have not rejected you. So do not fear, for I am with you; do not be dismayed, for I am your God. I will strengthen you and help you; I will uphold you with my righteous right hand. All who rage against you will surely be ashamed and disgraced; those who oppose you will be as nothing and perish."

Comment

Having summoned the nations and declared himself the Lord of history, God now gives a message to his covenant people. The term 'Israel my servant' is a term of comfort and endearment. In order to understand the full meaning of this message it has to be seen in context. After years of captivity in Babylon the people were cowed and dispirited. Most had lost their faith. 'God has forgotten us' they said, 'He has rejected us and no longer listens to our cries for help'.

The whole purpose of these chapters in Isaiah from 40 onwards is to restore the confidence of a broken people, to tell them of God's redeeming love; to proclaim his salvation and to assure them that however stubborn and sinful they had been God never ceases to love them.

This passage begins with a reminder of their history as the seed of Abraham, the friend of God. They had not chosen God, he had chosen them and called them to be his servant. The servant belonged to the household of the master and as such could expect to be provided for and protected.

That relationship was so strong that despite what had happened following the unfaithfulness of Israel, God had not rejected his people. God's love is not conditional upon ours. There is nothing that we can do to cause God to reject us. His love is unconditional and he is waiting to extend salvation to the worst of repentant sinners.

We get a little glimpse of the suffering of the Hebrew slaves in Babylon by reading Psalm 137, 'Our tormentors demanded songs of joy'. There was no joy in their hearts, only deep sorrow and a longing to see Jerusalem again and to be given the opportunity to rebuild her broken walls and to restore her marred beauty that had given rise to the mockery of pagan nations and brought disgrace to the name of the Lord.

'Do not fear, for I am with you' was the powerful message from the heart of God proclaimed by his prophet. 'Do not be dismayed for I am your God, I will strengthen you and help you; I will uphold you!' Then followed the promise that God would soon intervene to scatter the enemy and break the power of Babylon. 'Those who oppose you will be as nothing and perish'. The effect of this message upon a broken people must have been amazing beyond description. It transformed hopelessness to hope. It renewed faith and vision, it strengthened the resolve not to give way to despair, but to wait for the victory of God.

This same promise of salvation is valid today for all people through Messiah Jesus. God reassures us that he will never reject us. However far we stray from him, he never casts us off. The moment we cry out for help, he is beside us to wipe away the tears and to comfort, and strengthen and to restore us.

Prayer

Thank you, Lord, for this wonderful message. Help me to understand its meaning for me personally.

DO NOT BE AFRAID!

Isaiah 41: 12- 14 & 16b

Though you search for your enemies, you will not find them. Those who wage war against you will be as nothing at all. For I am the Lord, your God, who takes hold of your right hand and says to you, "Do not fear; I will help you. Do not be afraid, O worm Jacob, O little Israel, for I myself will help you," declares the Lord, your Redeemer, the Holy One of Israel. But you will rejoice in the Lord and glory in the Holy One of Israel.

Comment

These great promises of help continued to bring comfort and strength to those who were despairing of ever being freed from the shackles of Babylon. They are still a message of hope to all who are oppressed. God never ignores the prayers of his people. He awaits the right time and then swiftly moves to fulfil his promises.

For the people of Israel the promise that God had not forgotten them nor forsaken them must have come like fresh water in the desert to a weary traveller reaching the end of his endurance. The long years of separation from Jerusalem, compounded by the cruelty of their evil oppressors, had sapped the vitality from their faith and left only dull resignation. Year after year they had hoped for release, but help never came. Each time they celebrated Passover and greeted one another with, 'Next year in Jerusalem!' the words seemed more and more hollow.

Now, at last, God had raised up a prophet among his dispirited people to bring them a message of hope and joy. His message was in the great Isaianic tradition, using words and phrases that the great eighth century prophet had used in Jerusalem two hundred years earlier.

The phrase, 'The Holy One of Israel' occurs throughout the

book of Isaiah from chapter 1:4 to 60:14, but hardly anywhere else in the Bible - (twice in Jeremiah, once in Ezekiel and three times in the Psalms). It is characteristic of Isaiah of Jerusalem, who began his ministry with a personal experience of the holiness of God (Isaiah 6) that left a lasting impression upon him. He never used the word 'Redeemer' which is a characteristic of the writings of Isaiah of the Exile. He brings together the two phrases and speaks of 'Your Redeemer, the Holy One of Israel'.

The true God of Israel was not only the Holy One who was separated from the ordinary earthly material things of the world, but he was Israel's kinsman-redeemer. He was the one who was next-of-kin in the family and therefore had a solemn obligation to redeem from slavery those of his kin who had fallen into hard times. God's promise was that all those who sought to harm his people would be scattered, for the Lord would actually take hold of the right hand of his people and lead them to safety.

This is always God's promise to his people to all those who love him and put their trust in him. It is a message with special relevance for those who are oppressed or fearful, 'Do not be afraid', for even if you may feel as insignificant as a worm in the great natural world of creation, to God you are important. You are part of his beloved family. The promise of the kinsman-redeemer is that he will take you by the hand and lead you through whatever difficulties you may face. Therein lies the security of the people of God.

Prayer

Father, we are so thankful that you take us by the hand and lead us day by day. May this be a special experience today.

WATER IN THE DESERT

Isaiah 41: 17- 18 & 20
"The poor and needy search for water, but there is none;
their tongues are parched with thirst. But I the Lord will
answer them; I, the God of Israel, will not forsake them. I
will make rivers flow on barren heights, and springs within
the valleys. I will turn the desert into pools of water, and
the parched ground into springs. ... so that people may see
and know, may consider and understand, that the hand of
the Lord has done this, that the Holy One of Israel has
created it.

Comment

This is an important message for all who wish to go deeper in
understanding God's purposes for the life of each of his
people. It is always those who recognise that they are spiritually
poor and needy who come to God with a deep thirst, like
travellers through the desert reaching an oasis. Blessed are those
who hunger and thirst after the Lord.

It would be a mistake to interpret this passage as applying
literally to the physical conditions encountered by the Israelites
on the return from Babylon. They would not be crossing a
desert, but would follow the time-honoured route north from
Babylon across the Euphrates Valley and then south to enter
Israel through the Hazor Pass and through the Judean hills up to
Jerusalem. Water would not be a problem so this was not what
the prophet was saying.

The interpretation of this passage is spiritual, using figurative
language. The imagery is of God transforming the desert into a
fertile land. Verse 19, which we have not included in the reading,
lists seven trees - a perfect number for the renewed natural
environment - a kind of latter-day Garden of Eden. These
symbolised God's intention of renewing his people, taking them
from the humiliation and degradation of slavery to a people of

spiritual power who reflect the glory of their God.

The vision of the transformation of nature from desert to fertile land symbolises the renewal of Israel and leads the prophet to declare the purpose of God in calling Israel to be his servant through whom he will reveal himself to all the world. It is to enable all people to know that God alone has supernatural power. He is not like the pagan gods of the nations who have no power over nature. He has that power for he is the Creator and holds all the world in his hands.

When God raises up Israel, the nation despised by the world and rejected as powerless and insignificant, the transformation will be so remarkable that all nations will marvel. The final sentence of this passage has four verbs, one after the other, to show how important it is that all peoples shall learn the lesson of God's purposes in choosing Israel as his servant, a light to the Gentiles. They will SEE, KNOW, CONSIDER AND UNDERSTAND.

It is God's intention to reveal himself to others through the lives of those whom he calls into his service through his precious Son Jesus. God has actually chosen you as the one through whom he will reveal himself to your family, friends and acquaintances. He can only do this as you recognise your spiritual poverty and drink deeply from the well of living water, as the poor and needy search for water to quench their thirst.

Prayer

Lord, break the pride, or fear, that holds me back from allowing you to use me as you want.

DO SOMETHING!

Isaiah 41: 21- 24

"Present your case," says the Lord. "Set forth your arguments," says Jacob's King. "Bring in your idols to tell us what is going to happen. Tell us what the former things were, so that we may consider them and know their final outcome. Or declare to us the things to come, tell us what the future holds, so we may know that you are gods. Do something, whether good or bad, so that we will be dismayed and filled with fear. But you are less than nothing and your works are utterly worthless; he who chooses you is detestable."

Comment

There is a return here to a courtroom scene similar to the courtroom drama with which this chapter began. But in 41:1-4 those who were summoned to the seat of judgment were the nations, whereas here it is the gods who are called to account. Once again it is the God of Israel, here identified as 'Jacob's King', who is the judge calling for the accused to present their case.

There is no declaration here that these gods did not exist. The prophet was still preparing the way for such a revelation of absolute monotheism. The common belief among all the nations at that time linked the national fortunes and failures with the favour or displeasure of their gods. Babylon's claim was that their gods had triumphed over the God of Israel. This was difficult for the exiles to deny, although those who remembered the prophecies of Jeremiah would have known that God had predicted the exile through his prophets and they would have said that God had allowed the military defeat of his people due to their disobedience.

As part of restoring the faith of his people and their confidence in him, God now challenges the idols of the nations (the Babylonian idols in particular) to say what they have done in the past that has eternal consequences, or to give some revelation of the future with sufficient precision that it can be tested to see whether or not it is fulfilled.

Finally, in exasperation, Isaiah appealed to them to 'Do something' - Anything! Good or bad! The challenge was to do something supernatural so that the people could stand in awe of an exhibition of divine power.

This was not simply prophetic rhetoric. Isaiah's task was to restore the faith and confidence of the exiles in preparation for the mighty acts of deliverance that God had revealed to him. He knew it was in the near future, but the people were in no condition to be released and to face the rigours of the long trek home, or the demanding commitment of rebuilding the city of Jerusalem and the life of the nation. If the national life was to be rebuilt it had to be on the sure foundation of faith in God. It was therefore important that they knew in advance that God was raising up Cyrus the Persian to release his people, and in giving this foreknowledge he would break the power of the pagan gods over his own people and establish himself as the Lord of history.

For Christians this is the heart of the Gospel. Hundreds of years before the birth of Jesus, God predicted the coming of Messiah. Through his life, death and resurrection, he has defeated the powers of evil and broken their hold over his people. Through faith in Jesus we are set free from fear, and from the grip of the evil one, or any demonic powers, because nothing can separate us from the love of God through Jesus our Lord.

Prayer

Lord, help me to live in your freedom throughout this day.

TRUE PROPHECY

Isaiah 41: 25- 29
"I have stirred up one from the north, and he comes – one from the rising sun who calls on my name. He treads on rulers as if they were mortar, as if he were a potter treading the clay. Who told of this from the beginning, so we could know, or beforehand, so we could say, 'He was right'? No-one told of this, no-one foretold it, no-one heard any words from you. I was the first to tell Zion, 'Look, here they are!' I gave to Jerusalem a messenger of good tidings. I look but there is no-one – no-one among them to give counsel, no-one to give answer when I ask them. See, they are all false! Their deeds amount to nothing; their images are but wind and confusion."

Comment

This passage rounds up the courtroom scenes of chapter 41. It draws the logical conclusion there is only one true God, the God of Israel. The whole purpose of this chapter is to reach this conclusion. God himself speaks in the first person singular, 'I have stirred up'. He speaks as the judge summing up with a final speech before pronouncing the verdict. That verdict comes in the final sentence, 'They (the foreign gods) are all false! Their deeds amount to nothing'. These idols are just 'wind and confusion'.

It looks like a simple straightforward message, but in fact it is highly significant for Isaiah's theology. It is an affirmation that God is Lord of history. The phrase 'stirred up' is one regularly used by the prophets. In a vision given to Isaiah of Jerusalem concerning the end of Babylon he was shown that it would be the Medes, or Persians, who would deal the fatal blow; 'See, I will stir up against them the Medes' (Isaiah 13:17). Jeremiah also used a similar phrase when he was foreseeing the destruction of Babylon, 50:9, 51:1 and 51:11.

The statement that he would come upon Babylon from the north and the east (the rising of the sun) clearly indicates the territory of the Medes and refers to Cyrus. The statement, 'Who calls upon my name' has been a difficulty to biblical scholars for centuries since there is no historical evidence that Cyrus ever became a believer in the God of Israel. However, the Isaiah text in the Dead Sea Scrolls reads, 'And he called him by his name'. It would certainly make a lot of sense if we were to understand this passage as saying that God stirred up Cyrus and called him by his name. This would indicate the power that God exercises over foreign rulers. He knew them even though they did not know him.

None of the gods of Babylon had predicted such an event. They were powerless to give true prophecy because they were not gods at all, only dumb idols. True revelation comes from the one and only true God who is not only Lord of Creation, controlling the natural environment, but is also the one who directs the course of history to ensure that ultimately his purposes are worked out.

This same God is the Father of our Lord Jesus, the Messiah, who willingly laid down his life for us. All this was foretold to Isaiah the prophet long before the event. It is this God, who knows the end from the beginning, whom we can trust with our lives. He lives, therefore we who are alive in Christ live in the light and are nourished by the truth. The gods of this world are all false! 'Their images are but wind and confusion'. Do not be fooled by them, however attractive they may seem.

Prayer

Protect your people, O Lord, from the love of the false gods of this world that promise abundant riches and erotic pleasures. Reveal your truth to those who are in doubt or facing temptation.

THE SERVANT OF THE LORD

Isaiah 42: 1- 4
"Here is my servant, whom I uphold, my chosen one in whom I delight; I will put my Spirit on him and he will bring justice to the nations. He will not shout or cry out, or raise his voice in the streets. A bruised reed he will not break, and a smouldering wick he will not snuff out. In faithfulness he will bring forth justice; he will not falter or be discouraged till he establishes justice on earth. In his law the islands will put their hope."

Comment

This is the first of the great Servant Songs of Isaiah. There are seven songs; 42:1-4, 42:5-9, 49:1-6, 49:7-13, 50:4-9, 50:10-11 and 52:13 - 53:12. Strictly speaking they are not songs, but beautiful prophetic poems in honour of the Servant of the Lord who is called to serve all mankind.

Scholars have argued for centuries as to the identity of the Servant. Is it the nation Israel, or an individual referred to? The view taken in these pages is that the Servant is an individual, but that in himself he is representative of the idealised Israel. We take this view in the light of the revelation of the Messiahship of Jesus in the New Testament. There is a striking parallel between the Servant Songs and the Gospels. Both begin with the announcement of God's calling upon his Servant and the anointing with the Spirit. Both end with the Servant giving his life for the people whom he came to serve.

In this first Servant Song the emphasis is upon the anointing of the Servant, the task set before him and the way he will fulfil it. Unlike the call of the prophet, which is always an intensely personal and private experience with no witnesses, the anointing of a king was always a very public occasion, as when Samuel anointed Saul King of Israel and later did the same with David. The Servant is treated like a king. There is a very public announcement, 'Here is my Servant whom I uphold, my chosen one in whom I delight. I will put my Spirit on him'. The parallel with the baptism of Jesus is remarkable. When the Spirit descended upon him a voice was heard, 'This is my Son, whom I love, with him I am well pleased' (Matthew 3:17). Here, God testifies of the Servant, 'I will put my Spirit on him'.

The task given to the Servant was to 'bring justice to the nations', to 'bring forth justice with faithfulness and to 'establish justice on earth'. The way he was to do this would not be through violence, enforcing his will upon the people. He would not crush or snuff out the weak flickering flame of faith among his people. On the contrary he would act in faithfulness, respecting those who are bruised and powerless. Despite the fierceness of opposition, he would not falter in his determination to fulfil his mission to establish justice throughout the earth.

The Servant's teaching (Torah) will be recognised as the hope of the world. The reference to 'the islands' indicate the farthest known extremities of the world. Within the limited geography of that day the islands probably referred to the extreme west of Europe, ie the British Isles, although it is here used as a figure of speech rather than an actual place. The prophecy of this first Servant Song looks forward to the day when the Servant of the Lord will spread his influence throughout the world. Through the power of the Spirit of God upon him the word of God will reach all peoples. This great announcement prepared the way for John's Gospel prologue, 'In the beginning was the Word ... and the Word became flesh and made his dwelling among us' (John 1:1 and 14). This was the fulfilment of the vision revealed five hundred years earlier to the great prophet of the exile.

Prayer

Father, open the understanding of your people to recognise the way you have been working in the world from the beginning of time and help us each to know our place in your eternal purposes.

LIGHT FOR THE GENTILES

Isaiah 42: 5- 9
This is what God the Lord says – he who created the heavens and stretched them out, who spread out the earth and all that comes out of it, who gives breath to its people, and life to those who walk on it: "I, the Lord, have called you in righteousness; I will take hold of your hand. I will keep you and will make you to be a covenant for the people and a light for the Gentiles, to open eyes that are blind, to free captives from prison and to release from the dungeon those who sit in darkness. "I am the Lord; that is my name! I will not give my glory to another or my praise to idols. See, the former things have taken place, and new things I declare; before they spring into being I announce them to you."

Comment

The Servant Songs really form a whole message running right through the second half of the book of Isaiah. In this second of the seven-part message, God's purpose for the Servant is revealed. The Servant is addressed directly by God who first identifies himself as the Eternal Lord of Creation and the Giver of all Life. He then declares that he is the one who has called the Servant to act in the world as his agent. The Servant is given the assurance that he will not walk alone. God will be with him throughout his mission on earth. He promises to take him by the hand and uphold him. This close relationship between God and the Servant is expressed by Jesus when he acknowledges that the Son can do nothing without the Father. 'The Son can do nothing by himself; he can do only what he sees his Father doing' (John 5:19). Jesus makes this Servant relationship even more explicit when he says, 'I did not speak of my own accord, but the Father who sent me commanded me what to say and how to say it' (John 12:49).

The task given to the Servant was to be 'a covenant for the

people'. Scholars have argued about the identity of 'the people', but for those who accept that the Servant is the Messiah, and that Jesus is the Messiah, it is quite clear that 'the people' referred to here are the people of Israel. Jesus acknowledged that his mission was primarily to the people of Israel. He was called to be the fulfilment of the Law for them, to restore them to the fullness of God's covenant promises and blessings. God's intention always was that his covenant people would be used to reveal his word (Torah) and his nature and purposes to all the nations (Goyim). Hence here he reaffirms this intention to be fulfilled through the Servant who would be 'a light to the Gentiles' (Goyim).

The Servant was also called 'to open eyes that are blind, to free captives from prison and to release from the dungeon those that sit in darkness'. Jesus fully identified with this mission. In his message in the synagogue at Capernaum, when he read from Isaiah 61, he said, 'Today this scripture is fulfilled in your hearing' (Luke 4:21). Later, when John the Baptist's disciples came to him for reassurance that he was the Messiah, Jesus referred to the blind receiving their sight, the lame walking and the dead being raised (Luke 7:22). These were the outward signs of the divine power in Jesus, but his spiritual mission was to set people free from the bondage of sin. This was the real task of Messiah, the Servant of the Lord, to open eyes that were blinded by Satan and to bring release to those who struggle in the dungeons of darkness. It was to this mission of salvation that God called his Servant and anointed him with the power of his Spirit and promised his presence always.

This same mission, Jesus passed on to his disciples through the Great Commission, 'Go and make disciples of all nations'. With that command he also gave the promise, 'I am with you always, to the very end of the age' (Matthew 28:20). It was this same promise that had been given by the Father to the Son, and the same promise was given by God to the Servant in the beautiful Servant song that is our reading today.

Prayer
Lord, we thank you that you are an unchanging God who keeps his promises throughout all ages.

SING A NEW SONG

Isaiah 42: 10- 13
Sing to the Lord a new song, his praise from the ends of the
earth, you who go down to the sea, and all that is in it, you
islands, and all who live in them. Let the desert and its
towns raise their voices; let the settlements where Kedar
lives rejoice. Let the people of Sela sing for joy; let them
shout from the mountaintops. Let them give glory to the
Lord and proclaim his praise in the islands. The Lord will
march out like a mighty man, like a warrior he will stir up
his zeal; with a shout he will raise the battle cry and will
triumph over his enemies.

Comment

This is the first appearance of a new type of eschatalogical
hymn of praise that is peculiar to Isaiah of the exile. The
form is similar in some respects to the traditional psalms of Israel
such as Psalms 96 and 98 where the opening words are identical.
But the new element added by Isaiah to the command to praise is
the prophetic proclamation of what God will do in the day of the
Lord. The really wonderful and exciting element in this new
type of prophetic psalm is that the hymn of praise is linked with
a future event. Thus, not only Israel, but all the people of the
world, are commanded to praise God for an event that has not
yet taken place. They are to praise God for something he has not
yet done! That is faith!

This is the measure of Isaiah's confidence in God. It is also
the measure of his own absolute confidence in what he is hearing
from God. The prophet has no doubt that he has received an
amazing revelation from the Lord of his intention to change the
course of human history. God was intending to overthrow the
mighty Babylonian Empire. He would do this by 'stirring up'
Cyrus the Mede and establishing the supremacy of the Persian
Empire. Through Cyrus God would achieve his purpose of

releasing his people from Babylon and empowering them to return to the land of Israel and rebuild Jerusalem to his honour and glory.

This was not the first time that such confidence had been called for in the history of Israel. A notable example is found in 2 Chronicles 20 where King Jehoshaphat put the singers and musicians out in front of the army to lead songs of praise, thanking God for the victory that had not yet been won in a battle that had not yet been fought. That is faith! That is confidence in the Lord!

Isaiah was given an amazingly graphic and detailed revelation of God's purposes for his people and the effect upon world history this would have. He had absolute faith in God's ability to do what he had revealed to him. The first task was to prepare the dispirited people of Judah in exile in Babylon for what God wanted to do. Hence this great hymn of praise with its final verse declaring what God will do to break the power of the enemy over his people.

This is the kind of faith God is looking for today among his people. When Christians begin to understand and to evoke the power of prophetic praise, great will be the miracles that will occur, to the astonishment of the world! Prophetic praise is a demonstration of utter trust and confidence in the Lord. It is taking him at his word. It is declaring to the whole world the reality of something that has not yet happened as though it had already happened. It is standing on the promises of God.

This is the kind of faith that moves mountains, and it is the quality of faith that God is wanting to see in each of his children. It is not enough simply to repeat a creed, or to say a formal prayer. True faith requires spending time listening to God and having the confidence to stand on his promises.

Prayer
Lord, I believe. Help me in my unbelief.

TURNING DARKNESS INTO LIGHT

Isaiah 42: 14- 17
"For a long time I have kept silent, I have been quiet and held myself back. But now, like a woman in childbirth, I cry out, I gasp and pant. I will lay waste the mountains and hills and dry up all their vegetation; I will turn rivers into islands and dry up the pools. I will lead the blind by ways they have not known, along unfamiliar paths I will guide them; I will turn the darkness into light before them and make the rough places smooth. These are the things I will do; I will not forsake them. But those who trust in idols, who say to images, 'You are our gods,' will be turned back in utter shame."

Comment

There were many times in the history of Israel when the people cried out to God in complaint about his slowness to respond to their plight. The Psalms have many such references, such as, 'How long, O Lord? Will you hide yourself for ever?' (Psalm 89:46) and 'How long, O Lord? Will you be angry for ever?' (Psalm 79:5) These became part of what biblical scholars believe to have been 'community laments' which are repeated in many of the Psalms.

Here, Isaiah changes the format and repeats in the first person singular what he has heard from God. It is the divine admission that he has maintained silence for a long time. Jeremiah had warned and warned what the consequences of unbelief and idolatry would be. Those disastrous consequences had taken place in the destruction of Jerusalem and the deportation of the people to exile in Babylon. God had foretold this through his prophets and there had been nothing more to say for the period of the exile.

Now, however, the day of deliverance was about to dawn. God would keep quiet no longer. The period of gestation of the word of God was over. Like a woman coming to the end of her pregnancy, the climax is in the birth of a child, God was now crying out with a message of joy. The prophet was the herald of that message of new life. When God acts he will do amazing things. He will use his divine control of nature to confound the enemy. But he will also lead his own people gently along paths they have hitherto not trodden. This is to emphasise their helplessness and their utter dependence upon God. The people in exile were blind. They had been spiritually blinded by the terrible experience of exile from the land of Israel which made them believe they were exiled (cut off) from God. Their captors exulted in the triumph of the gods of Babylon over the God of Israel. The people had succumbed to this lie and consequently they were spiritually powerless. In fact, their spiritual blindness acted as a barrier to receiving any new revelation from God.

Blind people can do a great deal for themselves when they are in familiar surroundings. The greatest spiritual danger was that the exiles had become accustomed to living in Babylon. In order to break the spiritual grip of Babylon on his people, God was going to take them out into unfamiliar paths where they would be as dependent upon him as Israel had been in the desert after the exodus from Egypt. In this way God would 'turn the darkness into light before them'. At the same time he would make the rough places smooth so that his blind ones did not stumble as their eyes slowly opened with the new sight that he was giving to them.

This, of course, was no place for those who were still obsessed with the idols of Babylon. They would be turned back in disgrace. That is a strong word of warning to all who get caught up in the affairs and values of this world. God is working today to release his people from bondage to sin into the glorious liberty that he gives to us through the Gospel.

Prayer

Lighten our darkness, O Lord, we beseech thee.

BLIND AND DEAF

Isaiah 42: 18- 22
"Hear, you deaf; look, you blind, and see! Who is blind but my servant, and deaf like the messenger I send? Who is blind like the one committed to me, blind like the servant of the Lord? You have seen many things, but have paid no attention; your ears are open, but you hear nothing." It pleased the Lord for the sake of his righteousness to make his law great and glorious. But this is a people plundered and looted, all of them trapped in pits or hidden away in prisons. They have become plunder, with no-one to rescue them; they have been made loot, with no-one to say, "Send them back."

Comment

A common complaint among the exiles in Babylon was that God was deaf to the cries of his people and blind to their sufferings. Many had simply lost their faith and some had even turned to the local gods for succour. The general verdict of the community was that the covenant relationship with God was no longer valid. They were separated from the God of Israel who no longer heeded them or cared for them.

In this reading Isaiah forcefully turns the community lament back upon the people. He hears God complaining that his people are deaf and blind. They are the ones who are not acting as the servants of the Lord. Servants should be alert and watchful, waiting for their master's commands and ready to respond to his wishes. But Israel was deaf and blind to the word of God.

The great charge against Israel was that the people had learned nothing from the past. They had a rich history of revelation and teaching; they also had numerous occasions in their history when God had done amazing deeds and demonstrated his power as well as his great love for Israel. As a nation they had seen all these things, yet they had paid no attention. They had heard the words of the great prophets whom God had raised up in times of national crisis, yet they had heard nothing. At least, they had retained nothing, understood nothing, and carried nothing with them into the terrible situation of exile.

In Babylon they had 'become plunder with no-one to rescue them' (v22) at least this was their own lament, but it was not true. If only they would listen and 'pay close attention' to what God was saying to them they would understand both the reason for the exile and God's future plans for them. Isaiah then pressed home the very thing the exiles did not want to face 'Was it not the Lord against whom we have sinned' who handed Israel over to the plunderers? Until they accepted this unpalatable truth, they could never be used as the servant of God. They had to learn the lesson that servanthood demands absolute obedience.

The servant of the Lord cannot presume to know better than the master or to go his own way in times of prosperity. He cannot just ignore the teaching of the master and follow other teachers, going his own way when it suits him. No earthly master would tolerate such gross disloyalty and disobedience.

God warns his people time after time when we stray from his way, as he warned Israel many times in the years before the fall of Jerusalem. Are we, the people of God, any better today than the people of the exile? Is God charging his church today with being deaf and blind; with failing to learn from the past? Could it not be true that he is saying to each one of his children today, 'Which of you will listen to this or pay attention in time to come?'

Prayer

Father, open my ears that I may hear your word. Open my eyes that I may see your deeds. Open my mind that I may understand.

WALKING THROUGH FIRE

Isaiah 43: 1- 3
But now, this is what the Lord says – he who created you, O Jacob, he who formed you, O Israel: "Fear not, for I have redeemed you; I have summoned you by name; you are mine. When you pass through the waters, I will be with you; and when you pass through the rivers, they will not sweep over you. When you walk through the fire, you will not be burned; the flames will not set you ablaze. For I am the Lord, your God, the Holy One of Israel, your Saviour; I give Egypt for your ransom, Cush and Seba in your stead."

Comment

We come now to the heart of the message given to the people of the exile. It is expressed as a personal message, as though God were speaking to just one person, Jacob. This is intended to convey the intimacy between God and his chosen people.

It is not just the nation as an amorphous mass of humanity addressed here, but each individual is precious to the Lord. Hence the declaration, 'Fear not for I have redeemed you' expresses a one-to-one relationship. That phrase was quite ancient, going back hundreds of years in Hebrew family law. It referred to the act of a relative stepping in to pay off the debt, or 'redemption price' for a family member who had been imprisoned or enslaved through debt. We see evidence of this same phrase being used in the account of Ruth and her kinsman, Boaz, who rescued her from poverty and took her as his wife.

If we are really to understand the impact of this message upon the people of Judah in Babylon, we have to empty our minds from our highly spiritualised use of the term 'redemption' in modern Christian theology. It had a simple practical meaning in ancient Israel and was regularly used in family situations. To the exiles it meant that God had not forgotten or forsaken them.

They were still his people, even though they were in the most desperate and humiliating situation. They were still part of God's family and as Kinsman Redeemer he was acting to buy them back from Babylon.

The truly remarkable thing in this passage is that the verb is expressed in the 'perfect' tense, meaning that it is an action that has already been accomplished. 'I **have** redeemed you; I **have** summoned you by name'. Yet the people were still in captivity in Babylon. To the prophet the vision he had seen of God at work in the political turmoil of the rise and fall of empires was so real that he could speak of it in the past tense, as though it had already happened!

'You are mine' is the comforting personal assurance addressed collectively to the nations, but expressed individually to include each one of his people. The journey back to Jerusalem would be rough and tough, but God would be with them. Water and fire were symbols of difficulties and dangers, but nothing would be too great a problem for them. They would not be burned or destroyed, for God was in control of the nations and he, the Holy One of Israel, was their Saviour. He would ensure that as the warring empires of humanity battle for supremacy, his own people would be protected and would reach their homeland in safety.

It is a beautiful message of reassurance to each believer, to all who put their trust in God. We are not just an inconsequential part of a great mass of humanity. We are each one precious in God's sight. He says to each of us, 'You are mine! You belong to me in a personal relationship and I will never leave you alone!'

When we face dangers or very difficult situations, God's assurance is a personal guarantee of his love, 'When you pass through the waters, I will be with you ... When you walk through the fire you will not be burned.'

Prayer

Lord, I am so unworthy of your love. Help me to show my gratitude by conveying your love to others.

YOU ARE PRECIOUS

Isaiah 43: 4- 7

Since you are precious and honoured in my sight, and because I love you, I will give men in exchange for you, and people in exchange for your life. Do not be afraid, for I am with you; I will bring your children from the east and gather you from the west. I will say to the north, 'Give them up!' and to the south, 'Do not hold them back.' Bring my sons from afar and my daughters from the ends of the earth – everyone who is called by my name, whom I created for my glory, whom I formed and made.

Comment

This must rank high amongst the most beautiful verses in the Bible expressing the love of God. The words are in the first person singular. The prophet is reporting what he has heard from the mouth of the Lord about his unconditional love for his people.

The truly remarkable thing about this pronouncement is when it is seen in the light of the condition of the people. They were a bedraggled, powerless remnant of a once powerful and proud nation. Torn from their homeland and plunged into slavery in a foreign land, oppressed by a cruel people whose language they could not understand, they were a defeated and dispirited alien minority in Babylon, the capital of the mightiest empire so far known to the world.

It was amazing that the people of Judah had even managed to maintain their national identity. But the most stunning news was this pronouncement by the prophet. It is a staggering pronouncement when you think who is speaking and to whom the words are addressed. Here was the Lord who had created the whole universe, who sustained the stars in the sky and who held the nations in his hands as a drop in a bucket, the Lord of all creation was speaking to this tiny despised community and saying, 'You are precious and honoured in my sight'. It was a truly breaktaking declaration.

As if to underline the incredible difference between the Lord of history and the little group of displaced aliens, the pronouncement was followed by a promise, 'Because I love you I will give men in exchange for you and people in exchange for your life'. The clear meaning of this is that God was in control of the turbulent period of political change into which the nations were plunging. Through the international upheavals that were about to take place, God would ensure that his own beloved people were released from Babylon and returned to the land of their fathers. They would come from all corners of the Babylonian Empire and all this great regathering of those called by the name of the Lord would bring glory to God. This was his purpose in calling Israel to be his chosen people, to be a light to the nations and to reveal his love and purposes to the whole world.

To all those who feel worthless, despised and rejected by the world, this message of God's love is addressed today, through the Lord Jesus our Messiah. We all get depressed and discouraged at times. There are periods in life when nothing seems to go right and everything is hard. In such times we get tired and dispirited. That was the condition of the exiles in Babylon when God sent this message to them. He is sending the same message today to all who are finding life hard going. In our lowest moments, even though we may have sinned, as Israel had, the word of God is addressed to us, 'You are precious and honoured in my sight and I love you. Do not be afraid, for I am with you.'

Prayer
Lord, show me how I should be responding to your love.

NO OTHER GOD

Isaiah 43: 8- 10a
Lead out those who have eyes but are blind, who have ears but are deaf. All the nations gather together and the peoples assemble. Which of them foretold this and proclaimed to us the former things? Let them bring in their witnesses to prove they were right, so that others may hear and say, "It is true." "You are my witnesses," declares the Lord, "and my servant whom I have chosen, so that you may know and believe me and understand that I am he."

Comment

This is another trial scene like the courtroom dramas in 41:1-4 and 41:21-29. The new element in the scene is that Israel is called to be God's witness before this assembly of the nations.

It may seem strange to call witnesses who are blind and deaf! But this refers to hundreds of years that Israel has been a nation in a covenant relationship with God. As the people chosen by God to whom he would give his Torah, and through whom he would reveal his nature and purposes to the world, Israel was in a privileged position. As a nation they had a long history of observing, at first hand, the activity of God. They should have known and understood how he works. They should have known his requirements, above all, the loyalty he expected. They should have kept themselves clean from idols and the contamination of the world.

As a nation Israel had not been faithful. They had eyes that were blind, ears that were deaf. Because of this, they had ignored the warnings God had constantly sent to them through the prophets, and this had led to the tragic overthrow of Judah and the destruction of Jerusalem. Now, God was beginning to do a new thing. He was stirring up Cyrus the Mede and raising up the Persian Empire to overthrow Babylon. The fact that God was giving foreknowledge of this was a proof of his divinity. He knew all that was yet to happen as well as having been in control of all history.

The reason why Israel was called to witness God's words to the nations was so that, at last, eyes and ears would be opened. The whole purpose of this 'trial scene' was that Israel, the chosen servant of the Lord, 'May know and believe me and understand that I am he'. The phrase 'I AM' is of great significance here being the name of God first revealed to the fathers of Israel.

This is God's purpose, that his people should know him as the eternal God, the one and only true God; that they should not only know him but also believe him and understand him. God was giving his people a second chance. He was renewing them and restoring them.

This message lays the foundation for the Gospel that Jesus the Messiah preached. It is the assurance that however unfaithful or sinful we have been, God never ceases to love us. He is more ready to forgive us than we are to repent and to seek forgiveness.

God's desire is that each of his children should know him and believe him and understand him. That is why Jesus came in the flesh, so that we can understand the ways of God. Jesus said, 'I no longer call you servants, because a servant does not know his master's business. Instead, I have called you friends, for everything that I have learned of my Father I have made known to you' (John 15:15).

Prayer
Thank you, Lord, that you have made it possible for us to understand your ways and your purposes for our lives.

NO OTHER SAVIOUR

Isaiah 43: 10b- 13
**"Before me no god was formed, nor will there be one after
me. I, even I, am the Lord, and apart from me there is no
saviour. I have revealed and saved and proclaimed – I, and
not some foreign god among you. You are my witnesses,"
declares the Lord, "that I am God. Yes, and from ancient
days I am he. No-one can deliver out of my hand. When I
act, who can reverse it?"**

Comment

'Before me no God was formed, nor will there be one after
me.' This is probably the earliest statement of pure
monotheism in the history of world religion. From the time of
the eighth century onwards, the prophets of Israel had spoken of
the gods of the nations as false gods, eg Amos 2:4. Jeremiah got
very near to a monotheistic declaration with his rhetorical
question, 'Has a nation ever changed its gods? Yet they are not
gods at all' (Jeremiah 2:11); and his statement, 'Your children
have forsaken me and sworn by gods that are not gods' (Jeremiah
5:7). But none of the prophets actually stated that no other gods
existed. Isaiah of the Exile was the first.

It is hard for us today to recognise the impact that this
ground-breaking statement would have had upon the despised
little community of exiles in Babylon. It was probably beyond
their comprehension to be told that their God was the only divine
power in the universe; that he existed before the earth was
created, and that it was his hands that formed the earth and all
living creatures. Now God, speaking in the first person,
addressed them and called them to be his witnesses.

This is very similar to the words of Jesus just before the
Ascension, 'You will be my witnesses in Jerusalem, in all Judea
and Samaria and to the ends of the earth' (Acts 1:8). Here,
through Isaiah, the remnant of Israel was called to be God's

witnesses that he was not just the one true God among many gods, but that he was the only one - the whole universe was empty of divine beings apart from the God of Creation, the I AM, who had been in existence from ancient days and had revealed his name and his nature to the people of Israel so that they could be his witnesses to the world.

God had revealed himself to their forefathers, he had saved them in past generations when they had been threatened by other nations and he had proclaimed his word in their hearing. He had made his teaching known to the people and leaders of Israel. Now he was acting again, as in times past, on behalf of his people. Even though the present situation of the people in Babylon appeared utterly hopeless, they need have no fear, because God was their Saviour and he was putting his arms around his broken people to wrest them from the grip of the enemy. 'No-one can deliver out of my hand' he declared, 'When I act who can reverse it?'

There are many people who find it hard to believe that God has either the power or the will to deal with their present situation, particularly if it seems hopeless to human reason. But that is exactly how things seemed to the exiles in Babylon. They found this message hard to believe, but very soon afterwards they saw, with their own eyes, God fulfilling exactly what he had promised in one of the most amazing reversals of fortune in history.

God has not lost his power. He is the same God today as he was thousands of years ago. He is saying today to those of his people who feel helpless and hopeless, 'Apart from me there is no other Saviour. I have revealed and saved' in times past and now I am going to do it again - for you!

Prayer

Lord, increase my faith so that I can fully believe your word and embrace your good purposes for my life.

NO OTHER REDEEMER

Isaiah 43: 14- 17

This is what the Lord says – your Redeemer, the Holy One of Israel: "For your sake I will send to Babylon and bring down as fugitives all the Babylonians, in the ships in which they took pride. I am the Lord, your Holy One, Israel's Creator, your King." This is what the Lord says – he who made a way through the sea, a path through the mighty waters, who drew out the chariots and horses, the army and reinforcements together, and they lay there, never to rise again, extinguished, snuffed out like a wick.

Comment

All the build-up of the previous three chapters has been to prepare the way for this explicit prophecy, that God is about to destroy the empire of Babylon. The Babylonians (literally the Chaldeans) will leave the area in panic flight. They will jump on ships and flee down the Euphrates, so that the great ships in which they take pride will become the means of escape for fugitives. Isaiah was seeing the future conquest of Babylon by the Persians as clearly as though it had already taken place and he was simply reporting the details as a current news item.

The use of a combination of terms for the name of the Lord indicates the importance of this passage. He is the Holy One of Israel, the one who is different from all others, set apart from the world of humanity and material creatureliness. He is the Creator of Israel, the one who called the nation into being, who gave Jacob, the father of the nation, his name. He is the Lord who rules over Israel as their true King. Their earthly king had been defeated and destroyed, but the real King of Israel still lived. Finally, and most importantly for this passage, he is the Redeemer of Israel, the one who pays the redemption price to release people from bondage.

Following the announcement of God's impending action to overthrow Babylon, in case this seemed utterly fanciful to the exiles, the prophet reminded them of what God has done in the past. He recalled the days when Israel was in slavery in Egypt and God stepped into the scene in response to the cries of his people by breaking the power of Egypt.

This must have come as a timely reminder for the exiles that God was known to their forefathers as a redeemer. He had crushed mighty armies before and he could do it again. When Israel was faced with disaster after leaving Egypt and, finding their path to freedom blocked by the Red Sea, God had parted the waters in front of them and 'made a way through the sea'. It was God who 'drew out the chariots and horses'. In fact he led the whole Egyptian army and reinforcements together into the sea where they were extinguished, 'snuffed out like a wick'.

It is sometimes timely to be reminded of the great things God has done in the past, especially when we are labouring under difficulties and facing problems that seem insoluble. God is our Redeemer and he responds in love to those who put their trust in him. This was the condition of mankind when God sent the Lord Jesus to be our Redeemer. As Paul puts it, 'You see, at just the right time, when we were still powerless, Christ died for the ungodly' (Romans 5:6).

We sometimes forget that Jesus died for the ungodly - not for the righteous, but for the unrighteous. We can never be worthy of the love of God, but we should stop thinking that our unworthiness rules us out from his love. Our sinfulness, however great, cannot put us beyond his love or his power to act as our Redeemer.

Prayer

Thank you, Father, that you so loved the world as to send your Son. Help me to be open to all you want to do in my life today.

FORGET THE PAST

Isaiah 43: 18- 21

"Forget the former things; do not dwell on the past. See, I am doing a new thing! Now it springs up; do you not perceive it? I am making a way in the desert and streams in the wasteland. The wild animals honour me, the jackals and the owls, because I provide water in the desert and streams in the wasteland, to give drink to my people, my chosen, the people I formed for myself that they may proclaim my praise.

Comment

It does seem very strange that the prophet, who is so keen to remind the people of their history as the chosen people of God, should make such a statement as,'Forget the past'. It seems especially incongruous that in the previous verses there was a reminder of the exodus from Egypt and how God had made 'a way through the sea and a path through the mighty waters' (v16). This was the greatest of God's acts in the heritage of Israel which every Hebrew family was bidden to teach their children in order to ensure that it is passed on from one generation to the next.

Having outlined the greatest event in the history of Israel, the prophet then said, 'Now forget it! Don't dwell in the past!' Why would he make such an extraordinary statement? The reason was to prepare the way for God's dramatic announcement, 'See, I am going to do a new thing!'

God loves to do new things. He rarely repeats himself. He is continually moving on. He likes us to seek his will for us day by day and not just to assume that because he led us along a certain way in the past, we will always go the same way. Joshua tried that and it led to disaster. He enjoyed a great victory at Jericho by seeking the Lord for the strategy, then he moved on to Ai and did not ask the Lord for a plan and many men were killed as a result. When he did ask, he was given a completely different plan of action from that which succeeded at Jericho.

We have to wait until the next chapter (Isaiah 44:3) to find out what the new thing is that God was planning. But here the link was established with the predicted release of the exiles and their return to the land of Israel. On the occasion of the great exodus from Egypt, God had provided a dry path through the waters; now he was going to reverse that and provide water in a dry place. The interpretation of this has to be spiritual rather than a physical provision of streams of water in the desert since the exiles would not be crossing a desert in order to return home. The most likely explanation is that God was promising a renewing of the land of Israel and a spiritual renewal of the nation. He would transform both the land and its people.

The words, 'I will give drink to my people', means new life after the terrible experience of bondage in Babylon. Jesus promised to give drink to those who put their trust in him. He said that the water he would give would be like a spring of water 'welling up to eternal life' (John 4:14). This has a similar meaning. The remnant of Israel were the people whom God had formed for his own purposes and through them his name would be praised throughout the world.

The Lord delights in renewing his people, especially when they have come through a dry or difficult period, or testing experiences. He gives them the strength to come through and then gives the soft refreshing ministry of the Holy Spirit to renew vision and re-energise them for a period of service. He never leaves us in a spiritual vacuum. He comes to us bringing fresh vision, new life and hope for the future.

Prayer
Lord, only you can bring fresh vision, new life and hope for the future. Make me open to the ministry of your Holy Spirit so that I can receive all that you want to give to me.

THE JOY OF SERVICE

Isaiah 43: 22- 24

"Yet you have not called upon me, O Jacob, you have not wearied yourselves for me, O Israel. You have not brought me sheep for burnt offerings, nor honoured me with your sacrifices. I have not burdened you with grain offerings nor wearied you with demands for incense. You have not bought any fragrant calamus for me, or lavished on me the fat of your sacrifices. But you have burdened me with your sins and wearied me with your offences."

Comment

This passage can only be understood in the context of the exile in Babylon. Being separated from the land of Israel was a devastating experience. For most of the exiles it meant being separated from God. Their faith was not sufficiently mature to think of God in any other terms than territorial. Their theology was essentially polytheistic; many gods, each associated with a particular nation and territory. In being taken to Babylon they had left their God behind in the land of Judah.

Throughout the years of exile they must have discussed among themselves many thousands of times why the disaster had befallen the people of Judah and the holy city of Jerusalem. One of the explanations given was that they, or their forefathers, had offended God by not bringing the right offerings to the temple.

They had clearly never understood the message of the eighth century prophets. Isaiah of Jerusalem had thundered, 'The multitude of your sacrifices – what are they to me? says the Lord... Stop bringing meaningless offerings!' (Isaiah 1:11-13). The prophet now takes exactly the same stand. It was not due to a lack of presentations in the temple, but to a lack of the true spirit of worship. The offerings presented were formalities, they did not come from the hearts of the people, neither were they an expression of their love and devotion to the Lord. They were 'meaningless offerings' that did not bring honour to the name of God.

God's complaint here is that the people of Israel had not wearied themselves by making their chief objective in life to serve the Lord. Instead, they had wearied him, their God, by their sins. They had shown no loyalty or devotion to God. True, they had obeyed the letter of the law by bringing the prescribed sacrifices and by observing the festival days as given to them by Moses. But none of this had come from the hearts of the people. It was the observance of 'religion' rather than the outward expression of the deep love of God in the hearts of a people who put their trust in him.

It was the teaching of the great prophets of Israel that God hates 'religion'! That may seem a strange statement to those who are not familiar with the teaching of the prophets from Amos to Malachi. But if we are honest with ourselves we will know that it is quite possible to go to church and to repeat prayers, sing hymns, or songs of praise, and listen to familiar words, without it really touching our hearts.

In fact, we can listen without hearing, we can say prayers without praying, we can praise without worshipping. In just the same way the people of Israel could do all their religious practices without really worshipping God. They were still doing this in the temple at Jerusalem in the time of Jesus. Perhaps this is why he said that those who truly worship God must 'worship in spirit and in truth' (John 4:24).

Prayer

Lord, show your people how to worship you in spirit and in truth.
Make your presence a living reality so that we may know what you are
saying to us and our worship may be acceptable in your sight.

GOD'S FORGIVENESS

Isaiah 43: 25- 28

"I, even I, am he who blots out your transgressions, for my own sake, and remembers your sins no more. Review the past for me, let us argue the matter together; state the case for your innocence. Your first father sinned; your spokesmen rebelled against me. So I will disgrace the dignitaries of your temple, and I will consign Jacob to destruction and Israel to scorn."

Comment

This is another prophetic poem in the form of a trial speech. But unlike earlier courtroom dramas, where God called the nation and their gods to account, here it is Israel who is called to present her case before the Lord for judgment. Verses 22-28 are really all linked as a single oracle, so the charge that Israel's worship had not been an expression of the whole-hearted devotion of the people is what is in mind when God says, 'Review the past for me, let us argue the matter together; state the case for your innocence'.

Clearly, the people were grumbling that they (or their forefathers) had faithfully observed all the religious requirements. They had kept the festivals and presented regular burnt offerings and prayers in the temple. So why had God not protected them from the Babylonians? Why had he allowed Jerusalem to be destroyed? This was a regular complaint among the exiles and part of the laments of which there is plenty of evidence in the Psalms.

Psalm 74 is a good example of the cries of the exiles, 'Why have you rejected us for ever, O God?' There is a vivid (probably first-hand) description of the Babylonian soldiers destroying the temple and mocking God as 'they smashed all the carved panelling with their axes and hatchets' (v6). The exiles bore great resentment in their hearts towards God. Why had he allowed this disaster to come upon them? If he is a God of justice and love and mercy, as the prophets had taught, then where was the justice in his treatment of them? They were innocent, so they believed! But God had let them down by not protecting them from their enemies and by allowing Jerusalem to be destroyed. This was their complaint.

God invited them to state their case, but he reminded them of their history, going right back to Jacob, father of the nation, who was known as 'the deceiver'. He had cheated his brother from the moment of their birth, and was given the name of 'Israel' because of his struggles with God as Hosea had reminded them (Hosea 12:2-6). Deception and rebellion against God had been part of the spiritual heritage of the nation since its birth. This was the reason why God had allowed the dignitaries of the temple to be disgraced, the temple itself to be destroyed and the nation taken into slavery.

But right in the middle of this review of the past is the most beautiful promise of God's forgiveness. 'I am he who blots out your transgressions, for my own sake, and remembers your sins no more'. This is the measure of God's justice and faithfulness to an unfaithful people - *for his own sake*. For the sake of his name as a covenant keeping God, he forgives, and forgives utterly and completely. The slate is wiped clean, and he remembers our sins no more.

This is the heart of the Gospel. 'God so loved the world that he sent his only Son ...' (John 3:16). Jesus died for our sins, to set us free from the powerful bondage of the evil forces that have such a hold on us, and from the things that hold such an attraction for us. We only have to turn to him in penitence and he breaks the enemy's grip upon our lives, sets us free and fully forgives all that is past.

Prayer
'Amazing love, how can it be that thou my God shouldst die for me?'

OUTPOURING OF THE SPIRIT

Isaiah 44: 1- 3
"But now listen, O Jacob, my servant, Israel, whom I have chosen. This is what the Lord says – he who made you, who formed you in the womb, and who will help you: Do not be afraid, O Jacob, my servant, Jeshurun, whom I have chosen. For I will pour water on the thirsty land, and streams on the dry ground; I will pour out my Spirit on your offspring, and my blessing on your descendants.

Comment

Here at last is the answer to the statement in 43:19 where God promised to do a new thing! In that passage he had reminded Israel of the greatest act of salvation in her history when he had sent Moses to Pharaoh with the command to 'let my people go' and he had brought them out from Egypt in a mighty act of deliverance. Then he said, 'Forget the former things, do not dwell in the past. See I am doing a new thing'. After reminding them of God's greatest miracle in the nation's history, God said, 'Forget it!!'

What was this new thing God was planning which would make even the great exodus from Egypt pale into insignificance? What could be greater than the Exodus? It was this, 'I will pour out my Spirit on your offspring, and my blessing on your descendants'.

Isaiah was the first to be shown God's intention of making his Holy Spirit available to all people. Verses 1-5 are a complete unit, but here we are only dealing with the first three verses where the promise is to Israel and the descendants of Israel. In vs.4 and 5 we will see the completion of the prophecy when the blessing is extended to all nations through Israel. Here the promise is addressed specifically to Jacob, to the people of Israel, chosen to be in a covenant relationship with God, the nation whom God says he formed in the womb. This tender address is coupled with the words, 'Do not be afraid, O Jacob my servant,' and the term of endearment 'Jeshurun whom I have chosen.' Jeshurun, meaning 'the righteous one' is only used elsewhere in the Bible by Moses (Deuteronomy 32:15, 33:5 and 33:26).

In this extraordinary promise Isaiah was given foresight into the far distant future. He was shown one of the most significant events in the history of the world - the coming of the Holy Spirit. This happened at the birth of the church following the death and resurrection of Jesus the Messiah. The promise was that God would 'pour water on the thirsty land and streams on the dry ground'. This meant that God would refresh and renew the nation with a mighty outpouring of his Spirit.

The announcement to Isaiah of the Exile was in the form of a promise. That promise became a prophecy through the lips of Joel. He was told that God would pour out his Spirit upon all flesh (Joel 2:28). Most scholars believe that Joel was a post-exilic prophet which correlates with the promise here that the Spirit of God would be given to the 'offspring' of the exiles, and the blessings would be given to their 'descendants'.

This promise was not for the generation of the exiles, although it was dependent upon God fulfilling his promise to release the exiles and take them back to the land of Israel. It assumed that to be an accomplished fact and then looked to the future when God would act to establish the 'new covenant' relationship with Israel that Jeremiah had foreseen. He would make it possible for each individual believer to know him and to be in communion with him through the indwelling of the Holy Spirit. Jesus spoke of the Holy Spirit as the Comforter, and the Spirit of truth. He told his disciples to 'wait for the gift my Father promised' (Acts 1:4). The promise given to Isaiah, 'I will pour out my Spirit' was fulfilled on the day of Pentecost.

Prayer

Lord, we are so grateful that we not only have a Redeemer but that you have left your Holy Spirit until the work on earth is done.

THE GREAT HARVEST

Isaiah 44: 4- 5

They will spring up like grass in a meadow, like poplar trees by flowing streams. One will say, 'I belong to the Lord'; another will call himself by the name of Jacob; still another will write on his hand, 'The Lord's,' and will take the name Israel.

Comment

These two verses are part of the prophecy begun at verse 1 which foresaw the great outpouring of the Spirit of God. As we have already noted, the prophecy was not about the exiles in Babylon, but about their descendants. Isaiah was being shown events to take place in the distant future, long after the exile and the return of the people to the land of Israel.

In the reading today what is foreseen is the effect of the great outpouring of the Spirit. The prophet was shown two things of immense significance. The first was a great increase in the number of people belonging to the Lord. The second was that each individual would have a personal relationship with God.

In order to grasp the full import of what is being said in this prophecy it is essential to remember that it was given to the people in exile in Babylon as a follow-up to the prophecies of their return to the land of Israel, and as a declaration of God's intention for his people to be a light to the Gentiles. They were the nation through whom he had chosen to reveal himself to the world.

In the period after the exile God would refresh his people with an outpouring of his Spirit. This would lead to the two things in the passage we are studying. First, many people who are not belonging to the nation of Israel by birth will come and join the people who have received the Spirit of God. Multitudes will come, springing up 'like grass in a meadow, like poplar trees by flowing streams'. That is an indication of the rapid growth of the company of believers coming to join the Israelites who have received the Spirit of God.

Secondly, each of these new believers from other nations will take on the name of Israel. They will be part of the new Israel of God, and they will each have a personal relationship with the Lord. As slaves often had the name of their master engraved on their hands, or as intercessors often wrote the name of a loved one on the hands they held up in prayer, so the new believers would write the name of the Lord on their hands and become part of the family of God, his Israel.

Clearly the events described here were wonderfully fulfilled at Pentecost, following the death and resurrection of Jesus the Messiah. The 120 believers, all Hebrews, were filled with the Spirit of God and spilled out into the streets of Jerusalem as witnesses of the Lord Jesus. They were soon joined by people of many nations and 3000 were added to their number that day (Acts 2:41), following the public address given by Peter.

The great harvest foreseen in this prophecy is still taking place today as more and more people from nations all over the world are reached with the Gospel and respond to the message and receive the Spirit of God. The church today is growing at a faster rate than at any time since the early church.

Perhaps most significantly, we are seeing large numbers of Jews becoming believers in Jesus who is the Messiah of both Jew and Gentile. Could this be what Paul foresaw when he spoke of the Jews being as branches broken off through unbelief, but that the day would come when they would be 'grafted into their own olive tree!' (Romans 11:24). Surely those who form the true Israel of God are the believers in Jesus, both Jew and Gentile. This was what Isaiah foresaw.

Prayer

Father, your ways are wonderful, beyond our understanding, we can only praise you for the privilege of living in days that you revealed to your servants long ago.

NO OTHER ROCK

Isaiah 44: 6- 8

"This is what the Lord says – Israel's King and Redeemer, the Lord Almighty: I am the first and I am the last; apart from me there is no God. Who then is like me? Let him proclaim it. Let him declare and lay out before me what has happened since I established my ancient people, and what is yet to come – yes, let him foretell what will come. Do not tremble, do not be afraid. Did I not proclaim this and foretell it long ago? You are my witnesses. Is there any God besides me? No, there is no other Rock; I know not one."

Comment

This is the last of the 'trial scenes' that began with 41:1-4. The series of courtroom dramas in which the nations are challenged to recognise that God, the God of Israel, is the one and only true God, concludes with this final declaration of the uniqueness of God. Biblical scholars have problems with this passage because a plain interpretation of the words leads to the conclusion that Isaiah is teaching pure monotheism. This presents several difficulties. One is that historically many believe that the prophets did not reach this understanding as early as this in the history of Israel. Some believe that it is not until you come to New Testament Christianity that you get pure monotheism. Even Malachi still refers to 'foreign gods' (2:11) and he does not say that they do not exist.

The second difficulty is that Isaiah himself acknowledges the existence of other gods. In the trial scenes he calls upon the gods of the nations to present their case. In 41:23, the gods of the nations are challenged to foretell the future - or, in fact, to do *anything!* By doing something they would prove that they are gods. The assumption is that they cannot, because they are just blocks of wood or stone. Despite the reservations of some Bible scholars, there would appear to be good grounds for accepting that Isaiah *did* believe that there was no other god. Certainly his statement reporting God saying, 'Apart from me there is no other God' can mean that there is no god *comparable*. This could also be the interpretation of the question, 'Is there any God besides me?' But statements such as, 'I am the first and I am the last' indicate more than a mere uniqueness of character. It implies that there is no other god in existence and never has been.

God calls upon Israel, as his chosen people, to witness that there is no god like him. That is his purpose in electing Israel to be his people. They themselves can testify from their own history that God has spoken to them since they were first formed as a nation; that God has forewarned them of coming events and that he has provided for them, protected them and led them. This does not preclude the existence of other spiritual forces, such as demonic powers. Even Jesus acknowledged their existence, but it establishes the pre-eminence of the one true God who is not only the Creator of the universe, but is also Lord of history.

Moses used much the same reasoning when he reviewed the history of God's dealing with his people and asked, 'Has any god ever tried to take for himself one nation out of another nation, by testings, miraculous signs and wonders ... You were shown these things so that you might know that the Lord is God; besides him there is no other' (Deuteronomy 4:34-35). The phrase, 'There is no other rock' is a favourite phrase in the Psalms such as, 'You are my rock and my fortress' (71:3). Its earliest use in the Bible is in the prayer of Hannah as she presented the infant Samuel to the Lord at Shiloh (1 Samuel 2:2). The description of God as 'our Rock' really sums up the message of this passage. He is the steadfast one, who is completely dependable. He does not change. He is the same today as he was ten thousand years ago, and he can be absolutely trusted to keep his word. His love for his children never changes. He is our refuge and our strength, the Rock upon which we can rely under all circumstances.

Prayer
O Lord, you are my Rock, my fortress and my deliverer, my shield and my stronghold, in whom I take refuge. (From the Song of David in 2 Samuel 22:2-3)

SPIRITUAL BLINDNESS

Isaiah 44: 9a, 13a, 19- 20

All who make idols are nothing, and the things they treasure are worthless. The carpenter measures with a line and makes an outline with a marker; he roughs it out with chisels and marks it with compasses. No-one stops to think, no-one has the knowledge or understanding to say, "Half of it I used for fuel; I even baked bread over its coals, I roasted meat and I ate. Shall I make a detestable thing from what is left? Shall I bow down to a block of wood?" He feeds on ashes, a deluded heart misleads him; he cannot save himself, or say, "Is not this thing in my right hand a lie?"

Comment

This is a brilliant polemic against idolatry. The description in vv12-17 of the manufacture of idols is precise and beautifully expressed in detail, showing that the writer had observed at first hand the practice of the craftsman. The logical reasoning employed here to demolish the veracity of idolatry through the use of biting satire is probably the most powerful piece of writing on this subject in the entire Bible. We have only selected a few verses for our reading today, but the whole of vv9-20 should be read together to gain the full impact of this passage. Isaiah first describes a blacksmith at work shaping a metal image; then a carpenter; then how the wood was obtained; followed by the use of it; part for fuel, part for cooking, and the rest for shaping into an image. That image was then worshipped as a god! How absolutely ridiculous! Can these idolaters not see the absurdity of using the same block of wood for cooking, for fuel and for worship?

Some Bible scholars have criticised Isaiah for this, saying that he has not understood the nature of idolatry. He is only looking at the outward phenomena, they say, and failing to grasp the spiritual dynamics behind the practice of idolatry. In fact, this fails to do justice to the prophet. His intention was deliberately to expose the stupidity of idol worship by caricaturising the practice. The step-by-step manufacture of the image exaggerates the illogical basis of idolatry in the same way as a cartoon caricaturisation of a man highlights his prominent features through exaggeration.

The whole purpose behind this passage is not just to say how foolish it is to bow down to a block of wood, but to make the penetrating theological observation, 'a deluded heart misleads him'. That is Isaiah's incredible spiritual perception of the demonic nature of idolatry which gains such a supernatural hold on human beings that they are unable to exercise their reason. Their minds are deluded, their thinking is clouded. They are unable to see what should be obvious, even to a child, but they are powerless to break the grip upon their lives. It is like drugs, or alcohol, or smoking, or gambling - it becomes an obsession - a spiritual power that can only be broken by a greater spiritual power.

This is a spiritual truth of immense significance today. We can so easily dismiss this passage as having no relevance for us, but in so doing we miss the heart of Isaiah's message. We may not shape wood and metal into the image of a man and bow down to it as a god, but the whole of our industrialised, materialistic civilisation, is based upon exactly the same spiritual idolatry that Isaiah was debunking. The more our technology advances, the more dependent we become upon its physical products. However could we exist without cars and planes, TV, microwaves, computers, e-mail, the internet, mobile phones and all the paraphernalia and gadgetry to which we are addicted? Isaiah's answer is, 'Your mind is deluded, your heart misleads you. You cannot save yourself or say "Is not the thing in my right hand a lie?"' Is it not time to re-evaluate your life and to ask God to liberate you from the idolatry of modernity?

Prayer

Lord, I am surrounded by idolatry and powerful delusions. Open my mind to what is really important and may your precious Son set me free.

FULL FORGIVENESS

Isaiah 44: 21- 23

"Remember these things, O Jacob, for you are my servant, O Israel. I have made you, you are my servant; O Israel, I will not forget you. I have swept away your offences like a cloud, your sins like the morning mist. Return to me, for I have redeemed you." Sing for joy, O heavens, for the Lord has done this; shout aloud, O earth beneath. Burst into song, you mountains, you forests and all your trees, for the Lord has redeemed Jacob, he displays his glory in Israel.

Comment

This passage resumes the theme of 44:6-8 which ended with the declaration that 'there is no other Rock'. The polemic against idolatry was intended to show the utter stupidity of turning away to other gods. This was a great temptation facing the exiles after many years in Babylon, separated from the land of Israel by many hundreds of miles, and daily subjected to the indignity of forced labour. An even greater threat to their faith in God was the idolatrous practices of the Babylonians and their claims that their gods had overcome the God of Israel.

God's purpose in raising up Isaiah of the Exile was to counter this threat to the faith of his chosen people by reminding them of his deeds in the past, his great act of salvation in delivering their forefathers from Egypt. He was the Rock upon whom they could rely. All this was to prepare the people for the new act of deliverance from Babylon and to prepare the way for the restoration of the land of Israel, Jerusalem and, most importantly, of the nation itself.

An essential part of the message was the assurance of full forgiveness of past sins. There is nothing that can act as a greater barrier to God's purposes than our own refusal to recognise that we have been fully forgiven for past sins. The human mind has a strange way of retaining images of past sinful acts and throwing them back at us just when we are at our weakest moments. This is what was happening with the exiles. They were at their lowest point of self-esteem as statusless refugees, indentured servants in a foreign land, and in an alien culture. They continually told themselves that they richly deserved their fate because of past sins of their own and of their fathers. Inherited guilt can sometimes often be as devastating as personal guilt and even more destructive to faith.

God was longing to liberate his people from Babylon and to take them to the Promised Land, but first they had to be liberated from the negative effects of guilt. This beautiful message was intended to do just that. God reminded them that they were his people, he had made them, and he would never forget them. This was followed by the assurance, 'I have swept away your offences like a cloud, your sins like the morning mist,' and the appeal, 'Return to me, for I have redeemed you.'

When God forgives, he doesn't just put it in the back of a ledger to be brought up again at a later date. Full forgiveness means wiping the slate clean. That is what God does. He remembers our sins no more. It is as though they had never happened. It is, perhaps, because we find it so hard to do that with others, who sin against us, that we cannot accept it from God for ourselves. Sometimes we even find it hard to forgive ourselves! But God's ways are not our ways. We have to learn to take him at his word.

Such a wonderful act of full forgiveness requires the whole heavens and the earth to break forth into spontaneous praise, 'Sing for joy, O heavens, for the Lord has done this; shout aloud, O earth beneath. Burst into song, you mountains ...!' Can we refrain from joining in such praise?

Prayer
Father, put a new song of praise in my heart today.

RESTORING THE RUINS

Isaiah 44: 24, 26a, 27a 28
**This is what the Lord says – your Redeemer, who formed
you in the womb: "I am the Lord, who has made all things,
who alone stretched out the heavens, who spread out the
earth by myself, ... who carries out the words of his
servants and fulfils the predictions of his messengers ....
who says to the watery deep, 'Be dry' ... who says of Cyrus,
'He is my shepherd and will accomplish all that I please'; he
will say of Jerusalem, 'Let it be rebuilt', and of the temple,
'Let its foundations be laid'."**

Comment

We come now to the heart of Isaiah's prophecy. Everything
has been leading up to this from chapter 40, preparing the
way for the great announcement that Israel's exile is about to
end. The people first had to be prepared by the reassurance that
God had not forgotten them. He was not defeated. He was the
Creator of the universe, the Lord of history, who held the nations
in his hands. He had forgiven their sins and now he was about to
liberate his chosen people. Yes, they were still his chosen people.
He had formed them in the womb, and he was the one who had
the power to fulfil the predictions of his prophets.

At last came the almost incredible statement that the exiles
thought they would never hear, 'Jerusalem, it shall be inhabited.'
The towns of Judah would be rebuilt. Their ruins would be
restored. If this sounds impossible, God speaks to the 'watery
deep' and says, 'Be dry, and I will dry up your streams.' This is
simply to demonstrate that the God of creation, who has the
power to control all of nature, has the power to carry out his
purposes among the nations. He will fulfil his word.

The next question is, How is God going to release his people,
restore the land of Judah and rebuild Jerusalem? The answer is
the most astounding pronouncement ever to come from a

prophet of Israel. Speaking as the mouthpiece of God, Isaiah names Cyrus the Mede, who had recently become the head of the Persian Empire, 'He is my shepherd and will accomplish all that I please.'

It must have come as a profound shock to the Israelites of the exile to hear a pagan king referred to as a leader called by God to carry out his purposes. The prophecy was specific. Cyrus would not only declare that Jerusalem should be rebuilt, but also the temple itself. He would say, 'Let its foundations be laid.'

God loves to surprise his people with good things, with blessings far greater than they could even dare to imagine. It must have seemed utterly impossible that Jerusalem would ever be built again or the temple rise from its ruins. But God had promised it and soon the people would know that the God of Israel was indeed the God of the universe who had revealed to his servant the prophet what would happen. When the people saw Cyrus ride in triumph through the streets of Babylon they would know that their God reigns supreme.

So often we underestimate the goodness as well as the power of God. We think that if something very wonderful and pleasurable is offered to us, it cannot be God's will for us. How foolish! God loves to delight his children with good things. We think that if there are two alternatives facing us, one pleasant, the other a great burden, that God would not want us to enjoy life. We would have to opt for the unpleasant alternative. How foolish! How little do we understand the love of the Father who delights to give good things to his children.

Prayer
Father, help me to understand your ways and to accept your good gifts with thanksgiving.

GODLY SELF-CONFIDENCE

Isaiah 45: 1- 3
"This is what the Lord says to his anointed, to Cyrus, whose right hand I take hold of to subdue nations before him and to strip kings of their armour, to open doors before him so that gates will not be shut: I will go before you and will level the mountains; I will break down gates of bronze and cut through bars of iron. I will give you the treasures of darkness, riches stored in secret places, so that you may know that I am the Lord, the God of Israel, who summons you by name.

Comment

If the Israelites did not like God calling Cyrus his 'shepherd', they would have been really shocked to hear this foreign king referred to as the Lord's 'anointed'. This term was only used of kings of Israel, or priests and prophets of the Lord. At the time of Isaiah it did not yet have the meaning 'Messiah' that it had gained by New Testament times. But the phrase 'whose right hand I take hold of' would have been seen by the exiles as meaning that God was acknowledging the kingship of Cyrus.

The promises to Cyrus of the blessings God was going to bestow upon him would have presented further problems for the people. Why should God richly bless a foreign potentate? The promises of blessing went beyond going ahead of Cyrus to 'break down gates of bronze'. God even promised to give him 'the treasures of darkness, riches stored in secret places' interpreted by some as 'oil'! The whole Persian Gulf region has certainly been blessed by riches from the deep. Is this a reward for Cyrus' great generosity to Israel?

These promises must be seen in the light of all that had been said from chapter 40 onwards, emphasising that God is the Lord of Creation, and the Lord of history. In fact, in terms of biblical theology, all history is 'his-story' - the story of God's activity throughout the ages that human beings have inhabited the world. We are so conditioned by humanism that we only think in one dimension, that of human lives and human actions, and we see all events in the past through such a filter. If that filter were taken away, we would see how God has been at work despite wars and the wickedness of human beings. He is slowly working out his purposes to the day when he will draw all things to a final conclusion.

It was part of God's purpose to use Cyrus, the ambitious Persian leader, to break the power of the Chaldean Empire. He took Babylon without firing a shot - a most remarkable victory in the annals of warfare. Cyrus attributed this to the Babylonian god Marduk, having been outraged at the evil and injustices of the rulers of Babylon. This is recorded in the 'Cyrus Cylinder', a clay cylinder dating back to 538 BC, the time of the fall of Babylon, in which Cyrus attributed his victory to a foreign god, whom he called 'the Lord of the gods'.

There is an important spiritual principle here. It is that if God chooses to use someone for his purposes, he gives the gifts and the enabling, to ensure that the task succeeds. Many Christians miss the best that God wants for them through a lack of godly self-confidence. From the time of our conversion we are taught to have no confidence in the flesh. That is quite right, but all too often it leads to a lack of anointed self-confidence in carrying out the task God has called us to do. Godly self-confidence is putting your trust in the Lord, that he will give you the gifting and the resources to do what is necessary to fulfil your calling. Many believers are too timid to take God at his word. It is a mistaken form of piety, and even a false pride in 'having no confidence in the flesh'. God wants greater boldness in his servants - a willingness to trust him fully and to take risks for the Lord when he opens the doors.

Prayer

Lord, show me if there are any areas in my life where I am being too timid. Give me the boldness of your Holy Spirit to go through the doors that you open.

SUMMONED BY NAME

Isaiah 45: 4- 6a

For the sake of Jacob my servant, of Israel my chosen, I summon you by name and bestow on you a title of honour, though you do not acknowledge me. I am the Lord, and there is no other; apart from me there is no God. I will strengthen you, though you have not acknowledged me, so that from the rising of the sun to the place of its setting men may know there is none besides me.

Comment

This passage is one of the most significant in the entire Bible for biblical theology. Isaiah here takes us to greater depths than any of the prophets in an understanding of the nature of God and his purposes for human beings – the highest form of life in his creation. The whole passage is in the first person singular and he is therefore reporting what he has heard from the mouth of the Lord. It begins with a declaration of pure monotheism, 'Apart from me there is no God'.

Once again we are confronted with the great mystery of election. Why should the Creator God, the Lord of the universe, choose little Israel, a tiny despised Middle East tribe, to be his covenant people? Why did he choose Jacob and watch over his descendants, nurturing them into a nation and settling them in a land of their own? We begin to get an answer to that question when we ask the question the exiles would have been asking when they heard Isaiah's prophecy. Why did God choose Cyrus the Persian? The answer given here is not so that Cyrus would come to know God and acknowledge him, or that the Persian Empire should be the special recipient of God's favour. God promised to strengthen Cyrus, 'though you do not acknowledge me'.

This does not mean that God did not want Cyrus to know him, but simply that the time was not yet right for that to happen. The immediate reason for 'anointing' Cyrus was so that he could fulfil the task God desired – that is, God would use him to end the exile of Israel and return them to the land of Judah. This was necessary so that Israel could fulfil her calling as the covenant people of God through whom he would reveal himself to all the world. Thus the reason for choosing Cyrus was 'so that from the rising of the sun to the place of its setting men may know that there is none besides me.' This was the first step in God's plan of universal revelation, to let all people come to the understanding that there is only one God. This is what Paul is referring to in Romans 1: 18-23 where he says that 'what may be known about God is plain' for everyone to see. His eternal power and divine nature have been clearly seen, so people are without excuse for not acknowledging God. In releasing his people from the grip of Babylon God was preparing the way to send his own Son, the Messiah of Israel, to enable salvation to be extended to the whole human race.

Isaiah was shown God's purpose underlying the whole of creation from the time God separated light from darkness and brought order out of chaos. He saw the amazing truth that God has held all things in his hands from the beginning of time. Hence Cyrus was anointed for a one-off task, not an anointing for life, like the kings of Israel who were in a covenant relationship with God. Cyrus was not. He was simply being used by God to liberate Israel and to return them to the land, so that they could resume their calling as the people through whom he would send Messiah to reach all nations with his word.

God has a purpose for each individual as well as for nations. If he can 'summon by name' a pagan king like Cyrus who did not know him, how much more important it is for those who do know him to seek God's purpose for their lives. Slowly, but surely he directs the course of nations over the centuries. But our lifetimes are so short by comparison, which makes it very important to discover his will for using the gift and talents he has given to us. It is all too easy to waste years and to end our lives in regrets. The time to seek the Lord is NOW!

Prayer

Lord open my eyes to see the open doors you set before me and give me the courage to go forward in faith with my trust in you.

PROSPERITY OR DISASTER

Isaiah 45: 6b- 7
**I am the Lord, and there is no other. I form the light and
create darkness, I bring prosperity and create disaster; I, the
Lord, do all these things.**

Comment

Once again we have a statement of tremendous significance
for biblical theology. It begins with the same statement that
began verse 5, 'I am the Lord and there is no other'. It is
important to keep this in focus in order to understand what is
being said. The absolute sovereignty of God is the key to
understanding the mystery of the universe.

This verse creates enormous difficulties for theologians
because it implies that God is the author of evil as well as good.
'I form the light and create darkness, I bring prosperity and
create disaster.' The whole statement is in the first person
singular which means that God is the speaker and the prophet is
simply the reporter. Indeed, no one would dare to make such a
statement *about* God. The problem is to harmonise the statement
'I form the light *and create darkness*' with the Genesis 1: 3 account
of creation which says that God transformed the formless empty
darkness by creating light.

The same principle of creation is carried over into moral
precepts in that the Genesis 3 account of 'The Fall' shows evil
coming in to mar God's good and perfect creation. The Genesis
account shows evil irrupting not erupting. It irrupts into the
perfect harmony of God's creation and does not erupt out of the
work of God's hands. This is an important distinction. God is
not the author of evil.

In the light of this, God's statement that he creates light and
darkness, prosperity and disaster, cannot refer to moral good and
evil. The context is the declaration that God will use Cyrus the
Persian to overthrow Babylon and to restore Israel to their land.
This is not a moral judgment, although it implies a moral

judgment upon the wickedness of Babylon. It is a declaration of sovereign power, that God holds in his hands the destiny of nations. It is fully in line with Jeremiah 18 where God says 'If at any time I announce that a nation is to be uprooted, torn down and destroyed, and that nation repents …' (18: 7f).

This does not mean that God deliberately sends disaster upon individuals or nations. He does not have to! Usually our human wickedness brings its own reward, what Paul calls 'the wages of sin' (Romans 6: 23). Evil nations have no spiritual covering of protection over them so that their days are always numbered. When God's people sin they remove his covering and are exposed to the forces of darkness. He allows natural disasters to come upon nations, or plagues and diseases such as AIDS, BSE, or Foot and Mouth disease.

It is not a message that we like to hear but it should be seen as a counter to the dualism in popular evangelical theology that blames the devil for all adversity! Often, when we are faced with the collapse of things that we had hoped to see succeed, or with opposition from evil men, or even persecution, God says, 'I, the Lord, do all these things'. That is the last thing we want to hear, so we blame the devil instead of seeking what God is saying to us through difficult circumstances. The church often grows most vigorously through persecution. As servants of the Lord we grow more active through facing hardship and learning to overcome it in the power of the Holy Spirit.

No, of course, God does not want to send trouble upon his servants, but he *allows* it for our good, or perhaps because we have been too complacent and have not listened to him. He longs to send his 'shalom', peace and prosperity. But sometimes it is only when we face up to disaster by repenting and seeking the Lord in humility that we are able to enter into God's shalom.

Prayer

Lord, make me attentive. Teach me to listen to you so that I may understand your perfect will for my life.

POTTER AND CLAY

Isaiah 45: 8- 10
"You heavens above, rain down righteousness; let the clouds shower it down. Let the earth open wide, let salvation spring up, let righteousness grow with it; I, the Lord, have created it. Woe to him who quarrels with his Maker, to him who is but a potsherd among the potsherds on the ground. Does the clay say to the potter, 'What are you making?' Does your work say, 'He has no hands'? Woe to him who says to his father, 'What have you begotten?' or to his mother, 'What have you brought to birth?'"

Comment

This passage begins with a little hymn of praise. There is no agreement among scholars as to why it should be here. Does it form a conclusion to the preceding passage or an introduction to the next? No-one knows. Perhaps it just stands alone at this point simply to express praise to God for all the amazing things he was foretelling at that time, and a confidence that the whole of the created order of nature obeys his command.

The main message here is a dispute between God and Israel. They were his people. He had created them. They were his servants to do his bidding, that was why he had created Israel out of Jacob. Jacob was the clay, Israel was the pot; created for a particular purpose, as a jug for pouring water, or a jar for storage.

Just as the pot had no right to say to the potter, 'Why did you create me?' So Israel had no right to question God about his right to create a nation to be in a covenant relationship with himself. Isaiah of Jerusalem had used a similar argument when admonishing Judah for trying to hide their rebellious plans from the Lord, as though he did not have the ability to see them! How absurd! 'Can the pot say of the potter, "He knows nothing?"' (Isaiah 29:16). Jeremiah had carried this line of reasoning still farther when he was sent to the potter's shop and was given a powerful message from God, 'Like clay in the hand of the potter, so are you in my hand, O Israel' (Jeremiah 18:6).

The subject of this present dispute was the resistance of the exiles to the prophecy of Isaiah that God would use Cyrus the Persian as his 'anointed one' to liberate his people and to make possible the restoration of Jerusalem and the rebuilding of the temple. How could God use a pagan emperor who didn't even acknowledge him to rebuild, or even to cause to be rebuilt, his holy temple? It was absurd!

This was the reaction of the people, especially the pious among them, to the prophecies of Isaiah. They were dismissing them with scorn despite the great build-up by way of preparation in the pronouncements of the greatness of God as God of Creation and Lord of history. God's own answer was to remind them that it was he who had created them. They were the creation of his hands. 'Does the clay say to the potter "What are you making?"' Do children have a right to question their parents for bringing them to birth?

There are some people who are never satisfied with what they've got. They covet the good looks of others, or the better body shape, or strength of others. They wish they had the gifts, or talents, or resources of others. This kind of attitude inhibits growth. It stifles creativity and drains energy. It prevents God being able to use us to do the task for which he has gifted us.

The mistake is to think of ourselves as finished products. We are as clay in the hands of a skilled potter. God is continually fashioning us, but we can frustrate his good purposes by arguing with him instead of gladly and joyfully co-operating with him.

Prayer

Lord, make me a willing, obedient and joyful servant.

NOT FOR PRICE OR REWARD

Isaiah 45: 11- 13

"This is what the Lord says – the Holy One of Israel, and its Maker: Concerning things to come, do you question me about my children, or give me orders about the work of my hands? It is I who made the earth and created mankind upon it. My own hands stretched out the heavens; I marshalled their starry hosts. I will raise up Cyrus in my righteousness: I will make all his ways straight. He will rebuild my city and set my exiles free, but not for a price or reward, says the Lord Almighty."

Comment

Here we continue the same theme as in the previous verses in chapter 45. The focus is upon Cyrus the Mede, King of Anshan, a small province in the mighty Chaldean Empire, presently ruled over by Babylon. Cyrus was soon to extend his power right across the Babylonian Empire and beyond, to rule over the great Persian Empire, founding a new dynasty of the Medes and Persians. That empire would rule over the whole Middle East and eastern Europe until overthrown by Alexander the Great and the rise of the Greek Empire, which lasted until the Romans.

Cyrus was still only a minor, relatively unknown, provincial figure, at the time of Isaiah's prophecy. He was busy raising support to challenge the corrupt and oppressive regime of Babylon that dominated that part of the world. When he did finally march on Babylon, its rulers surrendered without a fight, and the local population actually hailed Cyrus as a liberator.

Isaiah foretold these incredible events which were revealed to him by God as a demonstration of his claim to be the one and only God, Creator of the world, and Lord of history. Here he takes the title 'the Holy One of Israel, and its Maker'. Once again this is a reminder to the exiles that he is the Father of the nation.

He protests at their temerity in questioning him about his children.

The exiles must have found this difficult because surely Israel was the only nation God had acknowledged as his own, therefore they and they alone were his children. But God deliberately chose to refer to Cyrus in those terms in order to underline his claim to be the Creator of all things in the universe and all the nations. Israel was in a special position as God's covenant people, although all men and women were his children. He therefore had the right to call Cyrus his son and to anoint him for a particular task.

It is interesting to note that nowhere does God call Cyrus his 'servant'. The servant is in a particular relationship with the master that implies a degree of permanence, not just a hired hand for the job. Servanthood involved rights and obligations. The master provided shelter, sustenance and protection for the servant, who in return served the master in whatever way was required. Cyrus was not a servant as Israel was the servant of the Lord. He was a hired hand whom God raised up to set the exiles free and to rebuild his city, but 'not for a price or reward'. Cyrus had his own motives. He was fulfilling his own ambitions, following his own agenda and not acknowledging God.

True servants of the Lord do receive reward for their services but the true servant is not motivated by the reward. That is the free gift of God. The motivating drive is the joy of service, the privilege of belonging to the Lord and being used by him. The reward is in the multitude of blessings that God delights to heap upon his servants whom, as Jesus said, he greatly favours by calling them 'his friends' (John 15:14).

Prayer

Lord, it is such a joy to be in your service, not seeking any reward, but simply for the privilege of belonging to you.

SPEAK THE TRUTH

Isaiah 45: 18- 19

For this is what the Lord says – he who created the heavens, he is God; he who fashioned and made the earth, he founded it; he did not create it to be empty, but formed it to be inhabited – he says: "I am the Lord, and there is no other. I have not spoken in secret, from somewhere in a land of darkness; I have not said to Jacob's descendants, 'Seek me in vain.' I, the Lord, speak the truth; I declare what is right."

Comment

The recurring theme throughout chapters 43-46 is the uniqueness of God. He is the Creator of all things and there is none like him. This passage begins with the same affirmation, 'He who created the heavens, he is God, he who fashioned and made the earth, he founded it.'

The importance of this for Israel in exile was to open their minds to understand what God was foretelling through Isaiah. He was not a mere territorial God like the gods of the nations, who were not gods at all, but were mere blocks of wood and stone. They could not answer the prayers of their worshippers, but God was able to save his people since he was the one true God.

All these declarations were designed to increase the faith of the people, to prepare them for release from Babylon and to prepare the way for the spiritual renewal of the nation, so that God could use them for his original purpose of being a 'light for the Gentiles', the conveyors of his word to the nations.

It is very important for us in the modern world to grasp the full import of the theology (the nature of God) that is being taught here. The biblical revelation of God is today being challenged by New Age concepts which teach the all-pervasiveness of God. He is said to inhabit the earth, to be present in nature, and in all creation. That is not the teaching of Isaiah!

In this passage God says that he founded the earth to be inhabited – that is, to be inhabited by the beings he had created – humans and animals and other living creatures, the work of his hands. He does not say that he himself inhabits the earth. Quite the contrary! God is shown throughout Scripture as being, 'wholly other' that is, he is totally separated from the material world. God is Spirit, and his worshippers must 'worship him in spirit and in truth' is the teaching of Jesus in John 4:24.

It is a lie to say that we are nearer to God in a garden than anywhere else on earth; it is sheer idolatry to worship 'mother nature' or any other part of God's creation. This passage emphasises that we do not have to engage in secret societies, mystery cults or delve into 'a land of darkness' in order to discover God. All these are spiritual perversions that may sound attractive and deceive many, but they do not show the way to God.

God is a God who speaks the truth, and declares what is right. He does not deceive or encourage people to seek him in vain. He has spoken plainly to Israel (Jacob's descendants) and all who truly seek him can find the truth revealed through those whom he has chosen and called to be his servants.

The restored Israel was to be the people of the Messiah through whom God would bring salvation to all nations. He has already sent his Messiah, Jesus who is the truth and the only way to the Father. Through Jesus we are able to know God as Abba, our loving Father who cares for each one of his children.

Prayer

Father, we thank you that you have sent the Lord Jesus, and that through him we have received your truth.

EVERY KNEE WILL BOW

Isaiah 45: 22- 25
**"Turn to me and be saved, all you ends of the earth; for I am
God, and there is no other. By myself I have sworn, my
mouth has uttered in all integrity a word that will not be
revoked: Before me every knee will bow; by me every
tongue will swear. They will say of me, 'In the Lord alone
are righteousness and strength.' All who have raged against
him will come to him and be put to shame. But in the Lord
all the descendants of Israel will be found righteous and
will exult."**

Comment

This is not strictly a 'Messianic prophecy' although it may refer
to events in the Messianic age, as Paul undoubtedly
interpreted it in Philippians 2:10-11. Paul, quoting from here, said
that the day would come when 'at the name of Jesus every knee
should bow ... and every tongue confess that Jesus Christ is Lord,
to the glory of God the Father.'

The wonderful thing about the work of the prophets of
ancient Israel is that they faithfully reported the words they were
given without knowing the full significance of what they were
declaring. This should be no surprise, since they were men of
their times with limited knowledge.

The immediate focus of Isaiah's attention was the plight of the
exiles in Babylon to whom he was called to prophesy. In this
passage he was seeing beyond the fulfilment of the prediction he
had already made of the downfall of Babylon. Now he invites the
vanquished oppressors, who are themselves fugitives, to come to
a great assembly where people from all nations will recognise
that the God of Israel, who foretold these momentous events, is
the only true God.

The prophet invites people from the ends of the earth to turn
to God because he is the only true God, 'There is no other.' This

one true God utters an oath that can never be revoked, 'Before me every knee will bow; by me every tongue will swear.' This does not mean a corporate mass turning of nations, but that every individual will acknowledge God as the only true God.

It is important to note that this is an individual decision and that everyone will say, 'In the Lord alone are righteousness and strength'. Thus each person on earth will acknowledge the justice and integrity of God and that he alone has power to fulfil his word. He is the Lord of the cosmos, Creator of all things and even those who have raged against him will be unable to resist acknowledging his Lordship.

It is the universal Kingdom of God that Isaiah was being shown. How much he understood of this no-one knows. It is impossible to say. He certainly saw the vanquished Babylon abandoning their gods and acknowledging that the God of Israel had foretold their defeat. But clearly he knew that he was being shown something of far greater significance, because he refers finally to 'all the descendants of Israel' rejoicing in a new righteousness. Paul picked up this theme in Philippians 2, seeing a clear reference to the work of salvation of Jesus the Messiah, although in Romans 14:11 he uses the same prophecy to refer to an end times judgment when each individual has to 'give an account of himself to God' (Romans 14:12).

For Christians this prophecy is special and gives reassurance that our God's purposes cannot fail. His kingdom *will* come and his will *will* be done on earth as in heaven. All believers in Jesus will be found righteous at their appearance before the Father - each one justified (made righteous) through faith in the Lord Jesus.

Prayer
Father, thank you that you have revealed your purpose of salvation for all people. May your word go out to all nations.

UPHELD AND CARRIED

Isaiah 46: 1- 4

Bel bows down, Nebo stoops low; their idols are borne by
beasts of burden. The images that are carried about are
burdensome, a burden for the weary. They stoop and bow
down together; unable to rescue the burden, they
themselves go off into captivity. "Listen to me, O house of
Jacob, all you who remain of the house of Israel, you whom
I have upheld since you were conceived, and have carried
since your birth. Even to your old age and grey hairs I am
he, I am he who will sustain you. I have made you and I
will carry you; I will sustain you and I will rescue you."

Comment

This is a vivid word picture of the fall of Babylon. Isaiah sees it
in a spiritual context of the vanquishing of the gods of
Babylon. He sees the wooden idols representing Bel and Nebo
being carted off in disgrace. Bel is the equivalent of Baal and
simply means 'lord'. His other name was Marduk, the patron god
of the empire. Nebo was his son. Traditionally the two gods were
paraded by their worshippers through the streets of Babylon at
the new year festival. The scene depicted in this prophecy is a
reversal of that ceremony. The fact that it did not happen in that
way at the conquest of Babylon by Cyrus in no way invalidates
the prophecy. Isaiah was a visionary prophet, he saw in pictures,
and this is his way of expressing the spiritual truth that he saw -
the humiliation of Babylon, despite all the pomp and ritual of
their pagan idolatry.

Cyrus, who was a polytheist, was quite happy to worship
Marduk, and actually claimed that Marduk had turned against
the current rulers of Babylon and had summoned him to conquer
the city. This actually authenticates Isaiah's prophecy and shows
that it was a genuine prediction of the fall of Babylon made some
time before the event. If it had been given afterwards the actual

events would have been described as they happened. It is a further proof of the genuineness of the prophecy that Isaiah's disciples, who preserved his words for prosperity, made no attempt to change the wording in the light of subsequent events. They clearly saw no problem! The description was of the spiritual fall of Babylon and the failure of her gods.

The contrast here is between the wooden idols of Babylon, that are unable to answer the prayers of the people, and the God of Israel. The wooden images have to be carried, whereas Israel's God carries his people! When they were conceived he carried them in the womb. He upheld them and carried them through the years in the desert, and he has carried them ever since, even to the upholding of the exiles through the terrible experience of separation from the land of Israel and from Jerusalem.

This is followed by a beautiful promise, 'Even to your old age and grey hairs I am he, I am he who will sustain you'. The repetition of the phrase 'I am' is a reminder of the name of God, I AM. God was saying to his people, as he spoke to the exiles in Egypt through Moses, 'I AM is promising to redeem you'. He follows this with the promise, 'I have made you and I will carry you, I will sustain you and I will rescue you'.

These are promises that are still valid today for every believer. Once we belong to the Father through Jesus we are his children in a special way. He rescues us when we are having problems. He carries us when we run out of strength and he sustains us when we are weary. If we will allow him, he will carry us right through our lives - even to old age and grey hairs.

Prayer
Father, thank you that through Jesus you have promised never to leave us. May I be conscious of your presence throughout today.

GOD'S PLAN

Isaiah 46: 10- 13
**I make known the end from the beginning, from ancient
times, what is still to come. I say: My purpose will stand,
and I will do all that I please. From the east I summon a
bird of prey; from a far-off land, a man to fulfil my purpose.
What I have said, that will I bring about; what I have
planned, that will I do. Listen to me, you stubborn-hearted,
you who are far from righteousness. I am bringing my
righteousness near, it is not far away; and my salvation will
not be delayed. I will grant salvation to Zion, my splendour
to Israel.**

Comment

This passage really begins at v8 with a direct address to the
exiles, the first since the beginning of chapter 40. They are
addressed as 'rebels', and told to listen carefully and to take the
message to heart. In v9 the name of God, I AM, is repeated,
reinforcing the solemnity of the pronouncement that comes from
the one who has been the God of Israel from the time of the
patriarchs. This is followed by the statement, 'I make known the
end from the beginning'.

The fact that God was able to foretell the future, that he sees
the end from the beginning, distinguishes him from the pagan
gods of the nations. He alone had known from ancient times
what was happening in Isaiah's day and what would happen in
the future, because he was in control of all nations. He was
steadily working out his purposes, despite the rebelliousness of
his own people and the ignorance of the nations who blindly
prayed to blocks of wood and stone.

'My purposes will stand and I will do all that I please' was the
message to the rebels who refused to believe the prophecies
brought by Isaiah that God had anointed Cyrus and was going to
use him as the saviour of Israel. Despite their wretched

conditions as slaves of their Babylonian overlords, these proud Israelites could not accept that this could be a word from God. The exiles saw it as humiliating that a foreigner should be used as their redeemer. God would never use an uncircumcised dog for such a purpose. Surely he would raise up another Moses to do dramatic things, with signs and wonders to force the Babylonians to let his people go!

In the face of these protests God addressed the exiles firmly, 'Listen to me you stubborn-hearted' and he repeated that he had summoned 'a bird of prey' to fulfil his purpose. This was his plan and he would not change it. 'What I have planned, that will I do'. This was the way he intended to accomplish the release of the exiles, which was only the first step in his plan to bring salvation to Israel, to restore and renew the nation through whom he intended to send his Messiah, to bring that salvation to all people in all nations.

How often do we frustrate God's plans by expecting some amazing demonstration of his power. We demand signs and wonders, whereas God likes to use the ordinary everyday things he has put into the world to carry out his plans. It is like someone refusing to go to the hospital for treatment while demanding that God performs a miraculous healing. Or a drowning man refusing to get into a lifeboat because he is expecting a miraculous rescue.

And God says, 'I have provided a skilled surgeon for you'. 'I sent that lifeboat for you. Do you not trust me to work out my plans for your good in my own way?'

Prayer

Lord, open my eyes to see your hand in the ordinary everyday things that I so often despise.

THE FALL OF BABYLON

Isaiah 47: 1- 2, 6- 7

"Go down, sit in the dust, Virgin Daughter of Babylon; sit on the ground without a throne, Daughter of the Babylonians. No more will you be called tender or delicate. Take millstones and grind flour; take off your veil. Lift up your skirts, bare your legs, and wade through the streams. I was angry with my people and desecrated my inheritance; I gave them into your hand, and you showed them no mercy. Even on the aged you laid a very heavy yoke. You said, 'I will continue forever – the eternal queen!' But you did not consider these things or reflect on what might happen.

Comment

With this passage we move into the climax of the message that began at chapter 40, the actual overthrow of Babylon. Isaiah had prepared the way and then spoken of the spiritual downfall of the gods of Babylon, but here we have the political and social fallout from the momentous events predicted. The prophecy foresees the humiliation of the people who had been oppressors of many nations. They had grown accustomed to enjoying the plunder of conquest and the luxury of being served by those they had enslaved. The name of Babylon was feared throughout the region and her people had become arrogant and filled with self-aggrandisement. Their status was now about to plummet.

Isaiah uses descriptive language to emphasise the sudden reversal of fortune that he sees overtaking the Babylonian people. They had been severe taskmasters to Israel, forcing the exiles to endure great hardship and physical labour. Now, the tables were about to turn and they themselves would be the ones toiling at the mills, grinding flour. The ladies who had boasted in their fine dresses would have to bare their legs and wade through streams to do the hard work now imposed upon them.

A new thought is added here. Although it has been hinted at before, now God spells it out that he was the one who handed his people over to Babylon. It was he who allowed his land and his city of Jerusalem to be desecrated. But the arrogant and cruel Babylonians have shown no mercy. They went far beyond what was the will and intention of God.

The Lord had handed over his people, withdrawing his protection over them, because of their disobedience, but Babylon had seized the opportunity to vent their merciless cruelty on Israel. In their blind arrogance they had assumed that they would rule the world for ever. They were destined to be 'the eternal queen'. This is probably a reference to Astarte, or Artemis, the Babylonian fertility goddess, whose worship was spreading across continents. She was referred to by Jeremiah who accused the people of Jerusalem of baking cakes with the image of the 'queen of heaven' on them (Jeremiah 7:18).

The charge against Babylon was that, in the arrogance of her people, no consideration was given to the real significance of her supremacy in the world of her day. The exercise of power, influence and authority carries responsibilities. Babylon ignored all these in an orgy of self-indulgence. In so doing she sealed her own fate. In due time God would ensure that she was overthrown and justice would be done.

In modern history a similar thing happened to Nazi Germany, whose cruelty to Jews makes the Babylonian exile look like a picnic. God hates cruelty and oppression. But the same principle applies to the exercise of power and authority in every sphere of life. We can be oppressors in our family, or place of work, or among our neighbours. When we misuse our position in life to the detriment of others, we offend God. We need to do what Babylon failed to do, that is to 'consider these things and reflect upon what might happen'.

Prayer
Lord, make me more thoughtful for others. Help me in the right exercise of the gifts and responsibilities you have given me.

SORCERY AND SEDUCTION

Isaiah 47: 8- 11a
**Now then, listen, you wanton creature, lounging in your
security and saying to yourself, 'I am, and there is none
besides me. I will never be a widow or suffer the loss of
children.' Both of these will overtake you in a moment, on a
single day: loss of children and widowhood. They will come
upon you in full measure, in spite of your many sorceries
and all your potent spells. You have trusted in your
wickedness and have said, 'No-one sees me.' Your wisdom
and knowledge mislead you when you say to yourself, 'I am,
and there is none besides me.' Disaster will come upon you,
and you will not know how to conjure it away.**

Comment

The use of the phrase 'I AM' twice in this passage gives a clue
to the significance of the charge being brought against
Babylon. It was more than the arrogance of the 'wanton creature,
lounging in your security'. They were actually arrogating to
themselves divine status. The rulers of Babylon were behaving
like gods. They were saying to themselves, 'I AM, and there is
none besides me'. Clearly, they had gone too far. They had over-
reached the authority God had granted them to subdue the
nations including Israel, his own covenant people. To set
themselves up as God put them on a direct collision course with
the Almighty. Isaiah saw that this had sealed the fate of Babylon.
Retribution would fall swiftly and with a finality that nothing
could halt. Loss of children and widowhood would be Babylon's
lot which her gods would be powerless to stop.

Babylon's offence against God was not only physical, through
her cruelty to Israel and the people she had conquered, but at
root it was spiritual. Babylon had actually been saying, 'I AM and
there is none besides me', the very words that God, the Creator of
the universe had said of himself! They had trusted in their own

wickedness, saying. 'No-one sees me'. The rulers of Babylon thought themselves to be above ethical requirements. They did not have to bring their actions before any outside bar of judgment, because their mystery cults were supreme. Their practices of magic and sorcery gave them supernatural knowledge and superhuman wisdom. But it was this reliance upon sorcery that would be their downfall. They were deceived in the spiritual realm, hence a disaster would come upon them no magical manipulation could ward off.

The danger of spiritual deception is just as great today as it was in the days of the Babylonian Empire. The gods of Babylon are still around in the modern world, ready to deceive the unwary and to suck them into their power. So often this can start in a seemingly harmless way by reading horoscopes and becoming interested in various forms of the supernatural. Many unbelievers have followed that route into the occult and witchcraft and Satanism.

For believers in the Lord Jesus, the spiritual temptations are more subtle and can be simply an over-emphasis upon the gifts of the Spirit leading to a 'me-centred spirituality'. It is all too easy to allow excitement with the manifestations of the Holy Spirit to distort our spiritual life by failure to recognise the reason why the gifts are given to the church. They are primarily given to the church! Not to individuals. They are for the building up of the body of Christ, and are intended to enable the church to fulfil the Great Commission and to reach all nations with the gospel.

The danger we face with spiritual powers of deception is that once we start to succumb to their attractions, deception begins to eat like a cancer in every part of life. So many Christian marriages that have broken down began in spiritual deception. The gods of Babylon entice their victims with seductive power, but once they have gained a foothold, corruption spreads through the entire body. There is only one safeguard; hold fast to the word of God, and raise the great shield of faith every day.

Prayer
Help me, Lord, to wear the whole armour of the Gospel throughout this day.

BURNED LIKE STUBBLE

Isaiah 47: 12- 14a
**Keep on, then, with your magic spells and with your many
sorceries, which you have laboured at since childhood.
Perhaps you will succeed, perhaps you will cause terror. All
the counsel you have received has only worn you out! Let
your astrologers come forward, those stargazers who make
predictions month by month, let them save you from what is
coming upon you. Surely they are like stubble; the fire will
burn them up. They cannot even save themselves from the
power of the flame.**

Comment

Babylon was not just the capital city of the Chaldean Empire, it
was a famous centre of culture and learning. Calling it the
Babylonian Empire was like calling the British Empire, the
'London Empire'. But such was the fame and dominance of the
city of Babylon that it was not unusual for the people of the
whole region to be known as 'Babylonians'. This was like calling
the Scots and the Welsh 'Londoners'!

The famous hanging gardens of Babylon was just one of the
wonders of the world of that day. People came from many
nations to consult the wise men of Babylon, who were a mixture
of astronomers and astrologers. For many years Babylon had
been a centre for the study of the stars. But their scientific study
did not stop at observation and noting the movement of the stars.
They went into interpretation and prediction. In this they were
influenced by the great variety of pagan practices in Babylon, city
of idolatry. Astrology was an important part of the life of the city.
The astrologers regularly published monthly predictions, saying
that the position of the stars portended good or evil, prosperity
or warnings.

Biblical scholars are divided as to whether Isaiah is here
scorning or taking the astrologers seriously. Clearly he believed

they were powerless to save Babylon from the coming invader who would overthrow the rulers of the city and humble its people. He challenges them to press on with their magic arts and sorceries to see if they could produce something to terrify the enemy. It was the belief of the sorcerers that they could manipulate nature to produce any result, but Isaiah knew this to be false. The God of Israel was the Creator of the cosmos and he alone controlled the world of natural phenomena.

Isaiah saw beyond the mere phenomenology (outward appearance) of magic and sorcery to the spiritual deception that was its source and therefore he warned that they were playing with fire which would eventually lead to their destruction. A living fire can be a great comfort on a cold day when you sit and warm yourself, but a forest fire out of control and blown by a strong wind burns up all in its path. This would be the end of the star-gazers of Babylon.

Our modern world is returning to the old superstitions of Babylon. Those who have no firm religious beliefs are wide open to deception. In nations like Britain, Europe and the USA, who have had the gospel for centuries, when they turn away from the truth they do not believe nothing, they believe anything!

Today, even leading politicians, presidents and royalty have been known to go to astrologers for predictions to help them in decision making. Many people use horoscopes for a similar purpose and some maternity hospitals even offer a service of life readings for new-born babies! We are not so far away from the primitive arts of paganism as we sometimes think, despite all our brilliant science and technology. Isaiah summed up with his last word in this chapter the sad plight of those who are caught up in this kind of deception. 'There is not one that can save you.'(v15) He meant, of course, the astrologers, not the Lord!

Prayer
Lord, we pray for those who are caught up in deception today, especially any of our own family, or friends, who do not know you. May your truth break into their lives.

STUBBORNNESS

Isaiah 48: 1, 4- 6a
Listen to this, O house of Jacob, you who are called by the name of Israel and come from the line of Judah, you who take oaths in the name of the Lord and invoke the God of Israel – but not in truth or righteousness – For I knew how stubborn you were; the sinews of your neck were iron, your forehead was bronze. Therefore I told you these things long ago; before they happened I announced them to you so that you could not say, 'My idols did them; my wooden image and metal god ordained them.' You have heard these things; look at them all. Will you not admit them?

Comment

The form of address to the exiles in this passage leaves no doubt about who is addressed - Jacob, Israel, Judah and, for good measure, the Jerusalemites! - 'You who call yourselves citizens of the holy city' (v2). This extended address is in order to emphasise the importance of what is being said. It is a message that God wants all his covenant people to hear and to understand. The message is a response to the cold way in which the exiles had responded to the glorious good news that God was about to release them from slavery. It would be natural to expect there would be great rejoicing among the exiles. This was what they and their fathers had longed to hear for many years.

Now that the announcement of God's impending action was declared, the people were grumbling and unwilling to accept it. The reason was because they simply could not countenance God using a despised foreigner as the means of their salvation. This all went back to the covenant with Moses, the conditions of which Israel had never understood. The eighth century prophets had consistently taught that Israel had not been chosen as God's special people because they were the greatest, or the most numerous, but because he wanted to raise up a people wholly dedicated to himself who would serve him in the world. He wanted a people through whom he could reveal his nature and his salvation to all nations.

Israel had always thought of themselves as God's special favourite and they could not accept a prophecy that accorded an 'anointing' by God on a pagan ruler. God's answer was to remind them that their fathers had always been stubborn and for this reason he had sent prophets in each generation to announce forthcoming events ahead of their taking place, so that there was no chance of people saying that their wooden idols had performed miracles for them. The final word is that they had heard all the great deeds of the Lord from their fathers, so they should now be prepared to 'declare them'. The word 'admit' in the NIV is a poor translation of *ta'idu* - literally 'attest'. They were God's witnesses to the world. They should be not only declaring his deeds of the past, but believing his word that Babylon was about to fall and declaring it to everybody. This was God's purpose in revealing it to them.

How often do we cling on to traditional ideas so that we are not open to anything new that God wants to do. Our stubbornness can be a hindrance to the fulfilment of God's purposes for his people and for our own individual lives. This is why it is so essential to learn to listen to God with discernment. Discernment comes by studying what God has done in the past. In this way we learn to understand the way he works and to know when he is speaking to us, even if it is revealing something new that we find surprising, or asking us to do something unexpected. By knowing what God has done in the past we can distinguish things that are in line with his character and his purposes. This enables us to reject the counterfeit voices that would deceive us and divert us into unfruitful paths. Jesus promised to send the Holy Spirit to guide us, 'When he, the Spirit of truth, comes, he will guide you into all truth' (John 16:13).

Prayer
Father, overcome my stubbornness and lead me to the truth through your Holy Spirit.

TESTED IN THE FURNACE

Isaiah 48: 6b- 7, 10- 11

From now on I will tell you of new things, of hidden things unknown to you. They are created now, and not long ago; you have not heard of them before today. So you cannot say, 'Yes, I knew of them.' See, I have refined you, though not as silver; I have tested you in the furnace of affliction. For my own sake, for my own sake, I do this. How can I let myself be defamed? I will not yield my glory to another.

Comment

Isaiah had been reminding the people of the great things God had done in times past and how he had foretold these things to the prophets of old. Now he announces, 'From now on I will tell you of new things'. No-one would be able to deny that God had revealed them to his people ahead of time. It is important to remember that Isaiah's message to the exiles is entirely about salvation, restoration and renewal. God was doing something new in the life of the nation. A new day was about to dawn, a new era in the unfolding purposes of God through his chosen people. The people needed to understand that God would not necessarily use methods he had used before. They should be open to him doing surprising things. Hence the message that he was going to use Cyrus, the Mede, as the means of releasing his people from the grip of Babylon should not surprise them.

God was going to return his people to the land of Israel for his own sake. The time had come to let the surrounding nations know that the God of Israel was not defeated. He had remained quiet for a long time whilst his people were being refined through the banishment from the land, but now was the time to redeem his own name in the sight of the pagan nations. He could not allow his name to be defamed any longer. God could not allow the gods of Babylon to go on taking the glory for the defeat of Israel. He would not yield his glory to another.

The outstanding part of this message for the exiles was the explanation of the purpose of their banishment from the land and their suffering in Babylon; 'See I have refined you, though not as silver'. The refiner of silver kept the molten metal at a high temperature and continually skimmed off the dross as it came to the surface. God says here that, although he had used the suffering of the people as a process of refining, he had not gone on and on until all the dross disappeared. This probably means there would have been very little of Israel left. It also is a measure of his own mercy and compassion. God sometimes allows his people to be 'tested in the furnace of affliction'. This is a phrase that came out of the time Israel had spent in Egypt. Moses referred to the Lord bringing his people 'out of the iron smelting furnace, out of Egypt, to be the people of his inheritance' (Deuteronomy 4:20). Now God was about to bring them out of the furnace of Babylon to be the people whom he could use to take his word to the world.

This may not be a message we want to hear, but it is a fact that, in order to prepare us for what he wants to accomplish in our lives, God sometimes has to allow us to go through testing times. When we can find the faith and courage to praise him in the midst of the furnace of affliction, then he knows that we are ready to be entrusted with great responsibilities of service. Paul speaks out of his own experience of God's sustaining power in all the suffering he endured on his missionary journeys. He says, 'We also rejoice in our sufferings, because we know that suffering produces perseverance; perseverance, character; and character, hope' (Romans 5:3-4). It is not easy to rejoice in the midst of suffering, but it sometimes helps to remember how the Lord Jesus suffered for us.

Prayer
Lord, when I go through testing times, help me to know that you are always with me.

IF ONLY ....!

Isaiah 48: 12, 17- 19
"Listen to me, O Jacob, Israel, whom I have called: I am he; I am the first and I am the last." This is what the Lord says – your Redeemer, the Holy One of Israel: "I am the Lord your God, who teaches you what is best for you, who directs you in the way you should go. If only you had paid attention to my commands, your peace would have been like a river, your righteousness like the waves of the sea. Your descendants would have been like the sand, your children like its numberless grains; their name would never be cut off nor destroyed from before me."

Comment

The reading begins with a command to listen. It is issued in the name God had given to Moses, 'I AM'. Here it is used three times, 'I AM he; I AM the first and I AM the last'. This is to emphasise the solemnity of the announcement. The verses omitted from the reading (13-16) reiterate what has been said a number of times in chapters 40-48, that the God of Israel is the Creator of the universe, he has foretold things that the idols cannot, he has chosen Cyrus as his instrument for the release of the exiles, and his word will be fulfilled. Isaiah adds that he has been sent by God with this message.

The message still related to the reluctance of the people to accept the good tidings sent to them and to embrace the salvation offered by God. He was not only speaking of the physical release of the captives from Babylon, but the spiritual renewal of the nation. This was much more important in serving the long-term purposes of God.

The direct message from God in this passage begins, 'I AM the Lord your God who teaches you what is best for you'. The reference here is to the Torah. The word 'torah' means 'teaching' or 'instruction' and the five books of the Torah, Genesis to

Deuteronomy, were given for the instruction of Israel in the right way of life for the nation. The Torah was given for Israel's benefit, not for condemnation. The teaching was to enable the nation to walk in God's blessings, to enjoy his shalom, and to experience true prosperity. But the history of the past showed only too clearly that the teaching had been ignored.

If only Israel had paid attention to the commands of the Lord, how great her prosperity and peace (shalom) would have been! This echoes the words of Psalm 81:8f, 'If you would but listen to me, O Israel! ... But my people would not listen to me; Israel would not submit to me. So I gave them over to their stubborn hearts to follow their own devices.' The psalmist continued, 'If my people would but listen to me, if Israel would follow my ways, how quickly would I subdue their enemies.'

Here through Isaiah God says, 'If only you had paid attention to my commands, your peace would have been like a river ... your descendants would have been like sand'. Peace and prosperity would have been the unbroken history of Israel, ... if only...! God would have ensured the protection of the nation and given them peace with their neighbours and family life would have been blessed. In Isaiah's day infant mortality was high and a large family was a sign of God's blessing.

The phrase 'if only' can be read in either the past or future tense. Here the context demands a past tense translation, but equally we can say that God says to us, 'If only you will heed my teaching, your peace and prosperity will be great.' He will watch over each member of our family and he will ensure that all things work together for our good. Despite setbacks or broken dreams, the Lord never leaves those who are faithful to him. The promise of Jesus is, 'I am with you always, to the very end of the age' (Matthew 28:20). That promise is still valid today.

Prayer
Lord, make me sensitive to your instruction and obedient to your teaching.

LEAVE BABYLON

Isaiah 48: 20- 22

**Leave Babylon, flee from the Babylonians! Announce this
with shouts of joy and proclaim it. Send it out to the ends
of the earth; say, "The Lord has redeemed his servant Jacob."
They did not thirst when he led them through the deserts;
he made water flow for them from the rock; he split the rock
and water gushed out. "There is no peace," says the Lord,
"for the wicked."**

Comment

'Leave Babylon, flee from the Chaldeans!' Isaiah's joy is
contagious. At last he has reached the summit of the first
part of his message, preparing the way for God's work of
renewing the nation and announcing the forthcoming Messiah
who will inaugurate a new era in God's purposes.

Babylon had not yet fallen. The people were not yet free to
leave the place of captivity, but the prophets always saw things
as they would be when God fulfilled the word he was revealing
to them. For Isaiah it was as though the gates of Babylon had
already been flung wide open and he could see the exiles
streaming through on their way back to Zion! Free at last! Free at
last!

Isaiah's unrestrained joy bubbled over. 'Proclaim it' he
shouted. 'Send it to the ends of the earth; say "The Lord has
redeemed his servant Jacob".' The message began with a clear
call to the exiles in the city of Babylon but, as so often happened
with the great prophets of Israel, they were carried from the
present into the near future, and then from the near future into
the far distant future.

Isaiah saw, not just the faithful remnant of Israel leave the city
of oppression, but the spiritual interpretation of the revelation he
was being given. Suddenly, the message took on an
eschatological nature. He saw the end times deliverance of the

messianic age when people of all nations, even to the ends of the earth, will respond to the call of Messiah, 'Come out of her! Leave Babylon!'

John, on the island of Patmos more than six hundred years later, had a similar revelation. He wrote, 'Then I heard another voice from heaven say: "Come out of her, my people, so that you will not share in her sins, so that you will not receive any of her plagues".' Then he saw the leaders of the nations, who had enjoyed the wickedness of Babylon, lamenting, 'Woe! Woe, O great city, O Babylon, city of power! In one hour your doom has come!' (Revelation 18:4 and 10).

This began as a call to the exiles who left Babylon in 539BC, but it developed into a call applicable to all who love the Lord to leave the world and seek to live in the presence of God. That does not mean that we can give up working and living in the system of the world's economy or social order. It does mean that we must reject the values of the world which are incompatible with the values of the Kingdom of God.

'You cannot serve two masters,' Jesus warned. You cannot both be a citizen of Babylon and a citizen of Zion. The two do not mix. You have to choose one or the other. Either you choose to allow the Spirit of God, the Holy Spirit, to guide and direct your life, or you will be driven by the spirit of Babylon, the spiritual forces of the world.

Isaiah saw that some of the exiles would stay in Babylon enjoying the pleasures of spiritual adultery, so he added, 'There is no peace, says the Lord, for the wicked'. How long will it be before God's children today heed the call to 'leave Babylon!'

Prayer

Lord, show me how this call applies to me.

TRUE SERVANTHOOD

Isaiah 49: 1- 4

Listen to me, you islands; hear this, you distant nations:
Before I was born the Lord called me; from my birth he has
made mention of my name. He made my mouth like a
sharpened sword, in the shadow of his hand he hid me; he
made me into a polished arrow and concealed me in his
quiver. He said to me, "You are my servant, Israel, in whom
I will display my splendour." But I said, "I have laboured
to no purpose; I have spent my strength in vain and for
nothing. Yet what is due me is in the Lord's hand, and my
reward is with my God."

Comment

This second Servant Song, (the first was in 42:1-9) begins a new
section of the book of Isaiah. Chapters 40-48 have been focused
upon the release of the captives from exile and their preparation for
return to the land of Israel. Babylon and Cyrus are not mentioned
again. The new theme in this section, chapters 49-55, centres around
the role of the Servant of the Lord, the restoration of Israel, and
how the Servant will accomplish his role.

The question inevitably arises, 'Who is the Servant of the Lord?
What is his identity? Is it Israel as a nation, or is it an individual?'
Or is there a third possibility, that the Servant is an ideal Israel?
Verses 1-6 should really be read as a whole, but for ease of
presentation we are taking them in two parts. There are three
speakers in the song; 'He (God) said to me' (v3); 'But I said' (v4);
and 'He says' (v6). It is perfectly clear from the first five verses that
the Servant is Israel, but in v6 he is told to restore Israel, and the
question arises, 'How can Israel restore Israel?'

In v1 the Servant gives his own testimony. It is to the whole
world, the farthest nations. He says that he was marked out by God
before even his birth, he was called for his task. His mouth was
prepared to deliver a message from God. He was destined and

prepared by God to be his spokesman to the nations. But he, the Servant, was not exposed to the world immediately. He was kept hidden by God awaiting the right time. In v3 the name of the Servant is revealed. It is 'Israel', 'He said to me, "You are my Servant, Israel, in whom I will display my splendour".' This is immediately followed by the response, 'But I said, I have laboured to no purpose; I have spent my strength in vain and for nothing.' This is the prophet speaking on behalf of the nation and looking back over the history of Israel. As a nation there had been so many times when they had been unfaithful to God. Time after time he had raised up judges and prophets to call them back to righteous ways and to rescue them from the consequences of their own sinfulness.

The history of Israel was one of confirming a covenant relationship with God, then dropping away into idolatry, suffering the consequences of God removing his cover of protection, crying out to God for help, then God helping them as repentance swept through the nation in their extremity. The recognition of this cycle of unfaithfulness and repentance brought a response in the final words of v4, 'Yet what is due to me is in the Lord's hand.' This is a kind of gloomy resignation rather than a glorious affirmation or determination to do the will of God. It is almost as though the speaker is saying that things would never be any different, Israel was an unredeemed people, unfit to be the Servant of the Lord. But this is precisely what the prophet was wanting to say as he began to move the message away from the mere physical restoration of the exiles to the spiritual restoration of the nation and the fulfilment of the purposes of God through his servant. That becomes clearer with each section in the following chapters.

We must wait until the next verses to discover the true identity of the Servant. The message of this section is that God never abandons his people however much we fail to live up to his intention for us. He does not reject us. He has a purpose for each one from the moment of our conception. Sometimes that remains hidden for a long time as he awaits the right circumstances, but once we are called, we are always a servant of the Lord.

Prayer

Lord, help me to fulfil your purpose for my life.

123

SALVATION FOR ALL

Isaiah 49: 5- 6

And now the Lord says – he who formed me in the womb to be his servant to bring Jacob back to him and gather Israel to himself, for I am honoured in the eyes of the Lord and my God has been my strength – he says: "It is too small a thing for you to be my servant to restore the tribes of Jacob and bring back those of Israel I have kept. I will also make you a light for the Gentiles, that you may bring my salvation to the ends of the earth."

Comment

There are two parts to this passage. In the first part the servant speaks, and in the second the speaker is the Lord. It is an important message that gives us further understanding of the true identity of the Servant of the Lord. These two verses are linked with vv1-4 and need to be read together.

We have already noted that this second Servant Song began with a testimony by the Servant addressed to all the nations of the world. This was followed by a gloomy recognition that as a nation Israel had consistently failed the Lord. But now there is a total change of mood. The Servant reports that despite past failures, God is honouring him, 'I am honoured in the eyes of the Lord.' He recognises that God has been his strength throughout all the vicissitudes of the history of Israel.

Now the message from God is that he is going to entrust the Servant with an even greater mission. Until now the task has been the restoration of Israel, and to bring back those who have remained faithful to the Lord. This restoration is not just a physical return of the people to the land but the spiritual restoration and renewal of the nation.   That is still the mission of the Servant, but added to that is the divine objective of making the Servant, 'a light for the Gentiles', the purpose of which, God says, is, 'that you may bring my salvation to the ends of the earth'. Here at last is the full extent of God's plan in calling the Servant into his service. The mission entrusted to him is no less than the salvation of the world. The revelation of such an incredible calling now puts us in a position to examine the question of the identity of the Servant.

From the time of God's call to Abraham to leave his homeland and tribal people and travel to Canaan, God had begun to carry out his plan of world salvation. With the conversion of Jacob following years of spiritual struggle culminating in a dramatic surrender, God began to form a new nation of which Jacob, now Israel, was the father. God's purpose in forming Israel as a people set apart from the other nations, a people separated (holy) to himself, was so that he could teach them the way of life he wanted them to follow. If only they had obeyed him and followed his teaching they would have learned to trust him completely. Then he could have revealed his nature and purposes to them and through them to all peoples.

The sad history of Israel's apostasy prevented this. God could not use them and finally he had withdrawn his cover of protection and allowed their enemies to triumph. But the exile in Babylon was used by God to prepare the way for a spiritually renewed nation to carry his word to the ends of the earth. Even at this stage God knew that they would fail to be his servant, so he began to prepare them with the expectation of a messiah - one of their own nation, who would be the idealised and personalised Israel. He would be totally obedient to God and would carry out his mission, first to bring a message of spiritual renewal to Israel and then to extend salvation to all peoples. Thus the Messiah, Jesus, is the true Servant of the Lord. As believers in the Lord Jesus, we are greatly privileged to be part of his body and therefore to be used by God to carry on the mission of taking the message of salvation to the ends of the earth - to be a light for the Gentiles.

Prayer
Lord, show me my part in the mission you have planned since the beginning of the world.

A NEW STATUS

Isaiah 49: 7
**This is what the Lord says – the Redeemer and Holy One of
Israel – to him who was despised and abhorred by the
nation, to the servant of rulers: "Kings will see you and rise
up, princes will see and bow down, because of the Lord,
who is faithful, the Holy One of Israel, who has chosen
you."**

Comment

This is a very difficult verse to interpret. There is almost
universal agreement that it stands alone. The crux of the
debate is whether this verse is linked with the preceding verses
or the following verses. The answer makes all the difference in
interpretation. The preceding verses are about the Servant and
the following verses are about the restoration of Israel. We get no
help from the use of the word 'Israel' as throughout chapters 49-
55 the nation is not referred to as 'Israel' but as 'Zion'.

The great question is, who is being referred to here? Is it the
servant or is it the nation Israel? Much depends on whether the
word 'nation' is in the singular or plural. NIV and KJV render
'nation' as in the Hebrew text. RSV and others render 'nations' as
in the Greek text (Septuagint LXX). If we read 'the one who was
despised and abhorred by the nation' then this clearly refers to
the Servant being rejected by Israel. But if we read '... abhorred
by the nations' this could be Israel in captivity in Babylon,
expelled from their own land, and despised by the surrounding
nations.

Clearly it is not easy to decide whether God is speaking to the
nation Israel or to the Servant as an individual. Once again, if we
follow the understanding of servanthood given in the last study
(vv5-8), we will conclude that the Servant is the idealised Israel
whom God eventually personalises in the figure of the Messiah.
The new status God bestows upon the ideal Israel, his servant, is

in stark contrast to the terrible condition of the remnant of Israel in exile. In Isaiah's day misfortune was always associated with spiritual condition, hence as a nation they were despised and rejected by other nations as spiritual outcasts whose God had rejected them or had been overcome by other gods.

Isaiah could have been looking forward to the day when all the nations would stand in awe of the God of Israel who had stood by his people in adversity and then had redeemed them and restored both land and people. But equally he may have foreseen the nation Israel rejecting the person of Messiah whom God would raise up as representative of the ideal nation. That rejection is foreseen as specifically referred to in chapter 53.

If we read this prophecy in the light of subsequent history, Isaiah was foreseeing Jesus the Messiah, who was rejected by the nation of Israel, and is today honoured by kings and princes who bow down before him. The one who was humiliated in his death on the cross has been greatly honoured in his risen life. All this displays the faithfulness of God.

God loves to honour his servants. To those who remain faithful to him despite trials and difficulties, and despite being despised and rejected by others, he delights to give a new status. He calls his servants, 'friends'. This was the teaching of Jesus (John 15:15) who said that through the ongoing ministry of the Holy Spirit his 'friends' would know their master's business.

To be able to understand what God is doing and how he is accomplishing his purposes is the privilege of all believers in Jesus. To be his people, part of his body, and to be acknowledged by him as a disciple whom he will one day present to his Father, is the highest status possible in this life.

Prayer
Thank you, Father, for the privilege of sharing in the new status you give to your people.

DAY OF SALVATION

Isaiah 49: 8- 9

This is what the Lord says: "In the time of my favour I will answer you, and in the day of salvation I will help you; I will keep you and will make you to be a covenant for the people, to restore the land and to reassign its desolate inheritances, to say to the captives, 'Come out,' and to those in darkness, 'Be free!' They will feed beside the roads and find pasture on every barren hill. "

Comment

We are on firmer ground here in saying that these verses refer to the restoration of Israel. But is it the physical restoration or the spiritual? Once again the question arises as to whether the person of the servant is intended to be read into these verses. Biblical scholars are almost unanimous in giving the answer, 'Yes'. And, in regard to the physical or spiritual restoration of Israel, the answer is not either/or, but both. We will try to unpack that a little.

Isaiah's starting point is the fact that Israel is in captivity in Babylon and that God has promised to release them. For them that will be a 'day of salvation'. But he sees beyond the return of the people to the land of Israel. He sees a deeper spiritual significance in what God is doing. He sees God's intention to raise up a people wholly dedicated to himself, fully trusting in him and rejecting the values of the world, while embracing the values of the Kingdom of God. He sees also that it is God's intention to use his holy people to reach the world with his teaching, to be 'a light for the Gentiles'.

Isaiah was also well aware of the sinfulness of his own people, Israel, and God gave him the revelation of his intention to use a saviour, his Messiah, to be the ideal Israel for accomplishing what the nation failed to do. So here in these verses there is both a physical and a spiritual message.

God is going to send a day of deliverance for the exiles and call them to leave the city of darkness and be free. He will restore them to the land and reassign them a dwelling-place - redoing the work of Joshua, 'In the time of my favour', reminiscent of the year of jubilee which was a time when land was restored to displaced families.

It is also important to note the deeper spiritual interpretation of these verses. The 'day of salvation' is a messianic concept. This is undoubtedly how it was interpreted by Paul who quoted it in 2 Corinthians 6:2 and added, 'I tell you, now is the time of God's favour, now is the day of salvation'. This was all in the context of the redeeming work of Christ who has reconciled sinful men and women to God. 'He died for all, that those who live should no longer live for themselves, but for him who died for them and was raised again' (2 Corinthians 5:15).

Isaiah was foreseeing this saving work of the Servant of the Lord who would be 'a covenant for the people'. He would say to those in captivity to sin 'come out' and 'to those in darkness "Be free!"'

This is the message that has been heard as good news by countless millions since it was first proclaimed by Peter on the feast of Pentecost, the day when all Israel was celebrating the first-fruits of harvest, and three thousand responded to the call to accept Jesus as Messiah.

This call is still going out today across the nations of the world and all those who belong to the covenant people of God, Jew and Gentile believers in Jesus, share in setting the captives free and rejoicing to see them enter into the new life in Christ.

Prayer
Lord, make me a faithful servant and give me the joy of seeing good fruit as I tell others the good news of Jesus.

GOD'S PROVISION

Isaiah 49: 10-12

They will neither hunger nor thirst, nor will the desert heat or the sun beat upon them. He who has compassion on them will guide them and lead them beside springs of water. I will turn all my mountains into roads, and my highways will be raised up. See, they will come from afar – some from the north, some from the west, some from the region of Aswan.

Comment

Once again this part of the prophecy has a double meaning. It applied first of all to the exiles in Babylon and their return, but it also has a wider application. The release of the exiles meant that they faced a long journey by foot, walking from Babylon to Jerusalem. It would be impossible to take with them sufficient food and drink for the long journey. They were going to have to find provision along the way. What God is promising here is that he will provide. Just as God provided for the people of the exodus from Egypt long ago, so he would provide for this new exodus.

Those who responded to the call to leave Babylon and were prepared to trust God for the long trek home would experience his compassion and his guidance. He would lead them like a shepherd 'beside springs of water'. The words here echo those of Psalm 23. But God would also make it possible for them to travel on mountain roads as well as across deserts, because he would be with them to guide and to protect them.

This does not mean that they would not have to cross mountains and deserts, but that he would be with them and would show them the best way. As he had provided for his people in the desert, sending a cloud by day and a pillar of fire by night, during the time of Moses, so he would provide guidance, as well as food and drink and protection, for the returning exiles.

It is significant to note that the exiles are not only returning to Babylon, but from far and wide. Some come from the north and some from the west as well as others from as far south as the southern borders of Egypt. So what is envisaged here is a world-wide movement of the people of God in response to the call of the Servant. That call went out to all nations as in 49:1, 'Listen to me, you islands; hear this, you distant nations.'

This prophecy foreshadows the great end times harvest of the Kingdom, when people of all nations will come to God through the Servant, his Messiah. The promise is not that they will never encounter mountains or desert places, but that God will be with them as their guide, protector and provider.

Sometimes we are faced with difficult decisions in responding to the call of God upon our lives, particularly if there are others dependent upon us. We try to see into the future, but it is not possible to enter upon a new phase in life with all the provision to see the way through to the end. That is not the way God works. It is his intention that we should trust him for each step of the way and not try to store up provision for a lifetime.

God delights to see his children trusting him. The spiritual principle upon which we can rely is that if God calls to a task he always ensures the provision. That does not guarantee us an easy path, or a 'free ride'. It does mean that when we respond to his call he will never leave us. In his love and compassion he will always be there beside us to lead and to provide.

Prayer

Thank you, Father, that you are the Good Shepherd who cares for the sheep of your pasture.

I WILL NEVER FORGET YOU

Isaiah 49: 13- 16
**Shout for joy, O heavens; rejoice, O earth; burst into song, O
mountains! For the Lord comforts his people and will have
compassion on his afflicted ones. But Zion said, "The Lord
has forsaken me, the Lord has forgotten me." Can a mother
forget the baby at her breast and have no compassion on the
child she has borne? Though she may forget, I will not
forget you! See, I have engraved you on the palms of my
hands; your walls are ever before me.**

Comment

In the midst of the message that Isaiah was proclaiming about
the release of the exiles, he also received revelation of God's
greater purposes and his plan of salvation for all peoples. He
broke off from the message with a great spontaneous shout of
praise. He just could not keep quiet! 'Shout for joy, O heavens;
rejoice, O earth; burst into song, O mountains!' Isaiah was so
overwhelmed by the majesty and wonder of the presence of God
and what he was hearing from him that he just could not keep
back the praise that welled up within him. That is real, genuine
praise! It is not the contrived praise we so often engage in
through formal hymns and prayers, or by turning up the volume
and trying to get a response through loud music or dancing.

'The Lord comforts his people and will have compassion on
his afflicted ones.' Isaiah saw that this was not just intended for
the exiles suffering humiliation and hard labour in Babylon, but
for all who love the Lord and who respond in faith to God's
servant whom he would raise up at the time of his favour. Then
he remembered the cool reception he had been getting from the
exiles who were unwilling to accept that God would use a
foreign king like Cyrus for his work of redemption. 'No' the
people said, this message cannot be from God because 'the Lord
has forsaken me, the Lord has forgotten me.' The sheer stubborn

stupidity of such a statement struck the prophet. He searched for the most obvious human attachment to use by way of illustration. 'Can a mother forget the baby at her breast?' There would be a physical reaction to remind her if she ever forgot to feed her baby.

The word of the Lord came to Isaiah, 'Though she may be forgetful, I will not forget you!' Although it is virtually impossible for a human mother to forget her new-born baby, even if she momentarily does forget in the midst of other family pressures, it is quite impossible for God to forget his children. He emphasises this by saying that Zion, Jerusalem, is never out of his mind. 'See, I have engraved you on the palms of my hands; your walls are ever before me.' The slave often had the name of his master written on his hand. This was a reversal; the master had the name of the servant on his hand. Of more significance was the practice of intercessors of writing the name of a loved one on their hands to lift them up in prayer before the Lord. Here God was saying that he had the name of Zion engraved on his hands. It was permanently there and could not be removed. The picture of Zion's broken walls was ever before God. This was to counter the lament of the people as recorded in Lamentations 5:20, 'Why do you always forget us? Why do you forsake us so long?'

To all those who feel lonely and rejected this message is a reminder that God never forgets us. Even though he allows us to go through many times of difficulty he never forsakes us, our situation is ever before him even as were the broken walls of Jerusalem. Clearly God was grieving over the devastation of the holy city and the plight of his people. He was awaiting the right moment to intervene and to bring salvation to his people. But even during the long period of waiting, he was still with them. It was impossible for him to forget them. It is just as impossible today for him to forget any of his children.

Prayer
Thank you, Father, for your promise, 'I will never forget you'. Make the reality of your presence clear to me today.

ABUNDANT BLESSINGS

Isaiah 49: 19- 21
**"Though you were ruined and made desolate and your land
laid waste, now you will be too small for your people, and
those who devoured you will be far away. The children
born during your bereavement will yet say in your hearing,
'This place is too small for us; give us more space to live in.'
Then you will say in your heart, 'Who bore me these? I was
bereaved and barren; I was exiled and rejected. Who
brought these up? I was left all alone, but these – where
have they come from?'"**

Comment

This is a beautiful picture of God's abundant blessings poured
out upon his people. Once again we have a prophecy that has
an immediate application and also looks to a long-term fulfilment
in the distant future. Its immediate application is to Jerusalem,
soon to be restored; while the long-term event is the end times
harvest of the Kingdom of God.

The opening verse of Lamentations speaks of the deserted city
'once so full of people' being 'like a widow' weeping bitterly
with none to comfort her as all her children were gone. This
prophecy reverses that and envisages the day when children
would be in Jerusalem again. It foresees the day when the city
will be too small for the great number of children, who will be
living in peace and security undisturbed by enemies.

Once the exiles are released and free to return to Zion the
ingathering of her people will be so great that the people will say,
'This place is too small for us; give us more space to live in.'
These will be the children born during Zion's bereavement,
during the exile in Babylon.

Jerusalem is spoken of as a woman bereaved, like the widow
of Lamentations 1:1 which is how the exiles thought of her. When
all her children, born during the exile, gathered to her, she would

say to herself, 'Where did all these come from?' 'Who bore me these?' She had never expected to have children again, being widowed and past the age of child bearing, but God was now abundantly blessing her. It was rather like Naomi taking the grandchild she never expected to see on her knee when Ruth delivered him into her lap (Ruth 4:16) and praising God for the kinsman-redeemer who had renewed her life in old age.

Jerusalem would say, 'I was bereaved and barren; I was exiled and rejected. Who brought these up? I was left all alone, but these - where have they come from?' This was God's good plan for Jerusalem. He was going to renew life and restore the nation as part of his purpose in preparing Israel to be the covenant people he had long planned. But the whole purpose of God could only be carried out by a holy people not filled with worldly desires, cleansed and purified. If the refining experience of exile did not accomplish this then the idealised Israel as the Servant of the Lord, would become the light for the Gentiles and raise up a new people of the covenant.

The day will come when people of all nations will flock to Zion, the city of God, and the family of the Redeemer will go on growing and growing. Even through the times of persecution and hardship the children of the Kingdom will multiply and come to the Lord.

God loves to bless his children, and those who put their trust in him are never disappointed. Unexpected blessings are poured into their lap. 'Where did these come from?' They came from the Lord, who delights to surprise you and to fill your cup to overflowing. 'O give thanks to the Lord for he is good; his love endures for ever' (Psalm 118:1).

Prayer
Thank you, Lord, for your abundant blessings.

YOU WILL NOT BE DISAPPOINTED

Isaiah 49: 22- 23
**This is what the Sovereign Lord says: "See, I will beckon to
the Gentiles, I will lift up my banner to the peoples; they
will bring your sons in their arms and carry your daughters
on their shoulders. Kings will be your foster fathers, and
their queens your nursing mothers. They will bow down
before you with their faces to the ground; they will lick the
dust at your feet. Then you will know that I am the Lord;
those who hope in me will not be disappointed."**

Comment

These verses provide an answer to the question in the previous
verse (v21) where Zion was seen as a bereaved woman
amazed that children were coming to her when she was barren,
widowed and childless. 'Where have they come from?' she asked.
The answer came, 'This is what the Sovereign Lord says ...'
God's answer was to say that he would summon the Gentiles to
bring back the scattered sons and daughters of Zion from far and
wide. 'See I will beckon to the Gentiles' is a reminder of the word
brought by Isaiah of Jerusalem that God would 'lift up a banner
for the distant nations, he whistles for those at the ends of the
earth' (Isaiah 5:26).

The raising of that banner was a sign of God taking the
battlefield against his own people. It was a strong warning to
Judah to repent and turn away from idolatry and wickedness
before God brought punishment upon them. The warning was
that he would do this as Sovereign Lord of the nations by
summoning a hostile nation from afar (Assyria) to come against
his own people.

Here there is a complete reversal. The banner of the Lord is a
symbol of peace and comfort rather than of war. His call to the
Gentile nations is to reverse the process of the exile. Those who
had been banished to far away places would be brought back by

their captors. They would bring Zion's sons back in their arms and carry her daughters on their shoulders.

There is a clear messianic link here. In Isaiah 11:10-12 the messianic figure is identified as 'the Root of Jesse' who will stand as a banner for the peoples. Two returns of exiles are recorded there. In the second the scattered people of Israel are gathered to the land from all parts of the world. Once again it is Messiah who raises a banner for the nations and draws all the scattered remnant to him.

This is what Isaiah of the Exile has in mind in this prophecy that he links with the Servant of the Lord. His mission will be to gather all those who truly belong to Israel to himself. Leaders of the nations will co-operate, kings and queens will bow before the Servant of the Lord and the new community of believers.

This is, of course, figurative language and does not mean that royalty will 'lick the dust' at the feet of believers. Rather, it envisages the acknowledgment by all the nations of the world that the messianic community has the truth, the true word of God. The objective of this is not to honour the community of believers, but to give glory to God. Then all people will know that there is only one true God, and that he is the God of ancient Israel who has watched over his people throughout the centuries and has now thrown open his kingdom to all believers.

Those whose hope is in him will not be disappointed. God never lets his people down. He delights to please and bless his children. To all those who put their trust in him he assures, 'Those who hope in me will not be disappointed'.

Prayer
Lord, increase my trust so that my hope is fully in you.

PULLING DOWN STRONGHOLDS

Isaiah 49: 24- 26

Can plunder be taken from warriors, or captives rescued from the fierce? But this is what the Lord says: "Yes, captives will be taken from warriors, and plunder retrieved from the fierce; I will contend with those who contend with you, and your children I will save. I will make your oppressors eat their own flesh; they will be drunk on their own blood, as with wine. Then all mankind will know that I, the Lord, am your Saviour, your Redeemer, the Mighty One of Jacob."

Comment

In the preceding verses of this chapter Isaiah has been dealing with questions raised by the exiles, largely centring on their charge against God that he had deserted them and forgotten them. God had answered this by saying that it was impossible for him to forget his people, but now they countered by querying whether he had the power to release them from slavery.

These verses deal with that subject. The question specifically is, 'Can plunder, or captives, be released from fierce warriors such as the Babylonians?' God's answer is a decisive 'Yes!' However fierce the enemy may be, God's power is greater. He not only has the power to set the captives free, but also to retrieve the plunder taken from Jerusalem and especially the holy vessels stolen from the temple.

God was preparing to contend with the oppressors of his people, to set them free and to safeguard the future of their children. The final statement about the fate of the oppressors should not be taken literally. It is figurative speech meaning that evil men bring trouble upon themselves. The violent provoke violence and those who live by the sword, or the gun, will die by the sword or gun. They bring upon themselves their own fate, reaping what they have sown.

God is a God of justice, so he stands back and allows the oppressors to turn upon each other. But his action, in vindicating the righteous, is a witness to all the nations that he is not powerless. He is the Saviour and Kinsman-Redeemer of Israel and he is also the 'mighty one' who has the power to accomplish what he purposes.

It needs to be remembered that this message is set within the servant passages in the prophecies of Isaiah. We should therefore look for a deeper spiritual message than the plain immediate assurance to the exiles of their release. God's purpose was more than merely setting the captives free. It was to prepare the way for the Servant (Israel, or the idealised personified Israel in the person of the Messiah) to bring light for the Gentiles (to all nations).

There are echoes in this passage in the teaching of Jesus. Isaiah asks, 'Can plunder be taken from warriors?' Jesus asked, 'Can anyone enter a strong man's house and carry off his possessions unless he first ties up the strong man?' (Matthew 12:29). This was part of Jesus' teaching on spiritual warfare and combating demonic powers. Paul said, 'We do not wage war as the world does'. He said that divine weapons are at our disposal to enable us to demolish strongholds (2 Corinthians 10:3-4).

Jesus had the power to cast out evil spirits and he gives that same power to those who put their trust in him. When we are assailed by temptation we are not left to succumb helplessly to the desires of the flesh or to attractive offers that we know to be wrong. We have the power of the Spirit of God within us to fight off the tempter. There are spiritual battles that all believers face in one way or another. Every time we call upon God for help he arms us with the power of the Holy Spirit to guarantee victory and our weakness brings glory to his name, our Redeemer, the Mighty One of Jacob.

Prayer

Come, Lord Jesus, and pull down any strongholds you see in my life.

NO-ONE TO ANSWER

Isaiah 50: 1- 3

This is what the Lord says: "Where is your mother's certificate of divorce with which I sent her away? Or to which of my creditors did I sell you? Because of your sins you were sold; because of your transgressions your mother was sent away. When I came, why was there no-one? When I called, why was there no-one to answer? Was my arm too short to ransom you? Do I lack the strength to rescue you? By a mere rebuke I dry up the sea, I turn rivers into a desert; their fish rot for lack of water and die of thirst. I clothe the sky with darkness and make sackcloth its covering."

Comment

This passage can only be understood in the context of the spiritual condition of the exiles and the mindset that had developed among them since the reduction of Jerusalem to ruins. The book of Lamentations gives revealing insights into this mindset. That is why in the Introduction we advise reading through Lamentations, ideally at a single reading, before embarking on these studies in Volume 2 of Isaiah.

One of the outstanding features of Lamentations is the constant reference to the fact that it was God who destroyed Jerusalem rather than Babylon. In fact, the word Babylon does not occur anywhere in the book of Lamentations. It is always acknowledged that it was *God's* action, 'Without pity the Lord has swallowed [us] up' (2:2); 'The Lord is like an enemy' (2:5); 'He has laid waste his dwelling like a garden' (2:6); 'The Lord has rejected his altar and abandoned his sanctuary. He has handed over to the enemy ...' (2:7). There is also a reference to Jerusalem having sinned (1:8) and a call to 'examine our ways' (3:40) and a complaint against the prophet (2:14). But the laments of the people were chiefly against God, rather than an acknowledgment of sin.

Here in Isaiah 50 the real cause of the destruction of Jerusalem is spelt out, 'Because of your sins you were sold'. The exiles were challenged to look at their mother's divorce certificate, and that would show the reason for her banishment. Jeremiah made this plain. He reported God saying, 'I gave faithless Israel her certificate of divorce and sent her away because of all her adulteries' (Jeremiah 3:8). Isaiah emphasises that God did not have to sell them because he was bankrupt, he sent his people away because of spiritual adultery (idolatry).

In this passage God also counters the complaints of the exiles by saying that he has been calling to them for a long time but they have not responded. 'When I called, why was there no-one to answer?' He had visited his people but they had ignored him. Did they really think that his arm could not reach to Babylon or that he lacked the strength to rescue them? He had the power to dry up the sea or to turn the sky to darkness. He was in total control of nature so he certainly had the power to deal with nations.

Before we pass judgment on the exiles for their unresponsiveness to God we should examine ourselves and the church of which we are a part. How often do we set aside time to listen to God? That does not mean praying, or praising or interceding. It does mean being quiet. There are many times when God says, 'Be quiet! Listen!' But there is no response - 'no-one to answer'. How few churches make time for quietness in public worship or even in small groups. We are afraid of silence. We have to fill every moment. We live in a culture of noise and activity. We think we have to turn up the amplifier for God to hear. Few church leaders teach people how to listen. Perhaps it is because we do not expect him to respond by speaking to us. That is why there is no answer when he calls and no response when he visits. Clearly we need to read the next two verses where Isaiah speaks of his own experience of listening to the Lord.

Prayer
Lord, give me a responsive heart. Make me open to your presence in a new way.

LISTENING TO GOD

Isaiah 50: 4- 6
The Sovereign Lord has given me an instructed tongue, to know the word that sustains the weary. He wakens me morning by morning, wakens my ear to listen like one being taught. The Sovereign Lord has opened my ears, and I have not been rebellious; I have not drawn back. I offered my back to those who beat me, my cheeks to those who pulled out my beard; I did not hide my face from mocking and spitting.

Comment

This is a key passage for all who want to deepen their spiritual lives. It is not clear whether this is the prophet Isaiah speaking or whether he is giving the testimony of the Servant. The passage is in the context of the Servant Songs, so such a connection cannot be ignored. But there is something very personal about the description here of a personal experience. Perhaps the two are not mutually exclusive and in thinking of the role of the Servant Isaiah speaks of his own experience of hearing from God.

'The Sovereign Lord has given me an instructed tongue.' This means that the words uttered by the prophet have their origin in God. The word of the Lord had been communicated to him. He was the mouthpiece of God, which is the definition of the 'prophet' that God gave to Moses. The arrangement God made between Aaron and his brother was that Moses would tell Aaron what God was saying if Aaron would be his spokesman. God defined this as 'your brother Aaron will be your prophet' (Exodus 7:1), i.e. your 'mouthpiece'.

Isaiah sees the whole world needing to hear the word of God - the word that 'sustains the weary'. Paul says something similar, 'The creation waits in eager expectation for the sons of God to be revealed' (Romans 8:19). Paul longs to see all believers prophesying (declaring the word of God) because 'everyone who prophesies speaks to men for their strengthening, encouragement and comfort' (1 Corinthians 14:1-3).

Isaiah reveals his own secret of hearing from God. He has trained himself to be receptive, to allow God to awaken him every morning with the eager expectation of hearing from God. This is the same eager expectation that a student/disciple has when sitting at the feet of a much respected and revered teacher. He hangs on to every word from the master. He is careful to be fully attentive so that he does not miss one word that is spoken to him.

Isaiah says this is how God has opened his ears in using those precious early morning hours before he engages in any human conversation or hears the opinions of men to pollute his thinking. Whilst his mind is still clear from the corrupting influences of the world, he opens up to the Lord. He probably did this before he even left his bed, but just lay quietly focusing upon God and allowing the Spirit of God to pervade his mind and to flood into his whole being.

There is a cost to the prophetic ministry. Here we see the blur between Isaiah's own ministry and that of the Servant of the Lord of which he is hearing from God and for whom he is the herald. 'I have not drawn back. I offered my back to those who beat me ... I did not hide my face from mocking or spitting.'

The Lord Jesus was to endure such treatment, as all the prophets had suffered before him. There is a cost to all discipleship. Those who truly desire to hear from God have to be willing to speak the word that he gives to them. He will not speak if that willingness is not there. Speaking the word of God draws out the mocking of unbelievers. The world always hates the word of the Lord and his servants suffer as their Master did.

Prayer
Lord, speak to me so that I can speak your living word to others, but first make me willing to bear the cost.

FACING PROBLEMS

Isaiah 50: 7- 9
Because the Sovereign Lord helps me, I will not be disgraced. Therefore have I set my face like flint, and I know I will not be put to shame. He who vindicates me is near. Who then will bring charges against me? Let us face each other! Who is my accuser? Let him confront me! It is the Sovereign Lord who helps me. Who is he that will condemn me? They will all wear out like a garment; the moths will eat them up.

Comment

The whole of chapter 50 is the third Servant Song but, as noted in the previous passage, some of Isaiah's own experience came into the description of the servant receiving the word of God. Here the focus is entirely upon the servant, but it picks up from v6, 'I offered my back to those who beat me ... I did not hide my face from mocking and spitting'.

The reason given for such exposure to violent opposition is because God is with the Servant, but the statement 'I will not be disgraced' seems at variance with his experience. This is followed by 'I know I will not be put to shame'. One would have thought that suffering, mocking and being spat upon would be being put to shame. Clearly there has to be a different meaning here.

The clue to the meaning of these statements is in v8, 'He who vindicates me is near. Who then will bring charges against me?' Isaiah is emphasising the sinlessness of the Servant. Although he is innocent of any offence (other than declaring the word of God) he offers his back to those who beat him and does not hide from his oppressors. The reason why he sets his face like flint when confronting opposition is because he knows that God is with him and that it is God who justifies or condemns, not human beings.

The Servant's confidence is in God alone. It is he who vindicates and God has already declared his Servant to be righteous. Therefore, 'Who is he who will condemn me?' If anyone does attack the Servant they seal their own doom. They will be like a worn-out garment full of moth holes that wears thinner and thinner until it is eaten up by maggots. That will be the fate of those who deliberately choose to oppose the work of the Servant.

It is important to note that the Servant's confidence is not in his own goodness, or strength, or righteousness, or any personal attributes. It is purely a confidence in God. He knows himself to be called by God. He knows he has kept himself pure by staying close to God and therefore he who vindicates him is close and any charges brought against him will finally be dismissed by God. It is in this sense that he is able to say with absolute confidence that he will not be put to shame.

When we face problems, or even fierce opposition as many believers are today, we have to make sure that our confidence is in the Lord. Christians in many parts of the world are suffering persecution and death today, at the hands of Muslim extremists and other haters of the Gospel. Other believers in secular societies face subtler forms of persecution or opposition.

Whatever the problems we face, provided we keep close to the Lord, and continue to put on the whole armour of God to resist the temptations of the world gaining a hold in our lives, we can have absolute confidence that the Lord will vindicate his servants. We can set our faces like flint and know that we will not be put to shame. The Lord will find a way of vindicating those whom he has declared to be righteous - having a righteousness, not of our own merit, but through what he has done for us.

Prayer

Lord, draw me closer to you so that your righteousness shines through my life.

RELYING ON GOD

Isaiah 50: 10- 11

Who among you fears the Lord and obeys the word of his servant? Let him who walks in the dark, who has no light, trust in the name of the Lord and rely on his God. But now, all you who light fires and provide yourselves with flaming torches, go, walk in the light of your fires and of the torches you have set ablaze. This is what you shall receive from my hand: You will lie down in torment.

Comment

This is the final part of the third Servant Song. Isaiah is here seeing the spiritual significance of the impending release of the captives and the restoration of the people of Israel. Just as God was about to use Cyrus to accomplish the first part of this mission in a physical sense, which was good news and liberation for the exiles, so the mission of the Servant would be good news and liberation from sin for the world. God had promised that Israel - or the idealised Israel in the form of the Servant - would be light for the Gentiles, so this passage picks up that theme.

This is a message of encouragement to those who respond to the mission of the Servant. It is particularly addressed to those who are in trouble, or who recognise their need. The message is, 'Let him who walks in the dark, who has no light, trust in the name of the Lord and rely on his God.'

The message was initially focused upon the hopeless situation of the exiles who saw no light at the end of the tunnel of their suffering in Babylon. They were exhorted to trust God. They could rely on him to come to their aid and to rescue them from their distress. But this led the prophet on to the real message of the Servant who was being raised up by God to liberate the suffering and oppressed people of the world.

Suffering and oppression is seen here not simply as physical, but its root is in human sin. This is what the Servant will deal with. He is the one who will bring light to the darkest places of the world. The prologue of John's Gospel (John 1:1-18) beautifully expresses the mission of the Messiah that Isaiah was foreseeing here. John saw in the birth of Jesus, 'The true light that gives light to every man was coming into the world' (v9).

The second part of this passage gives the contrast. Those who reject the true light brought by the Servant create their own light. They believe that their own wisdom, the wisdom of the world, is superior to the wisdom of God. Their light is brighter and blazes more spectacularly than the light of the Lord. They prefer doing things their way.

The prophet here foresees their end, they 'will lie down in torment'. The end result of sin, of rejecting the light, is darkness and suffering. This can be seen all around us today in the gathering clouds of violence from evil men, in the suffering of multitudes through sexually transmitted diseases, as well as the suffering brought about by broken relationships, broken trust, broken hearts, broken lives. Sin pays terrible wages.

But the good news is that the light has come into the world. The light shines in the darkness and the darkness cannot overcome it. It is there, gleaming bright, for those who will open their eyes and see. The light does not bring condemnation, but liberty, new life, joy and freedom to all those willing to take the risk of trusting Jesus, the Servant of the Lord. All who 'trust in the name of the Lord' and rely upon God will walk as children of the light and experience the joy of the Lord.

Prayer
Lord, help me to walk in the light as you are in the light.

LOOK TO THE ROCK

Isaiah 51: 1- 3
"Listen to me, you who pursue righteousness and who seek the Lord: Look to the rock from which you were cut and to the quarry from which you were hewn; look to Abraham, your father, and to Sarah, who gave you birth. When I called him he was but one, and I blessed him and made him many. The Lord will surely comfort Zion and will look with compassion on all her ruins; he will make her deserts like Eden, her wastelands like the garden of the Lord. Joy and gladness will be found in her, thanksgiving and the sound of singing.

Comment

The end of the third Servant Song is followed here by an appeal to the exiles. The appeal is addressed to those who have remained faithful to the Lord, to the remnant who try to keep themselves from the corrupting influence of Babylon. That corruption and idolatry was all around them and its spiritual contamination was subtle and intrusive. Therefore, those who were wanting to be faithful to God actually had actively to 'pursue righteousness'.

It would have been all too easy to drift off into compromise with the standards of Babylon, where wickedness and oppression encouraged cheating and lying, and where the fertility cults of the goddess Artemis offered attractive comforts. But there was a faithful remnant who sat by the rivers of Babylon and wept, remembering Zion. 'If I forget you, O Jerusalem' they said, 'may my right hand forget its skill. May my tongue cling to the roof of my mouth ...' (Psalm 137:5-6). The faith of the remnant was being sorely tested by the long delay in God fulfilling his promised release. It is always the faithful who suffer most. Those who had accepted the values of Babylon, compromised with the world, were no longer bothered about Jerusalem. They had settled for the temporal pleasures wherever they could find them. Here, the faithful are told not to give up hope. They were encouraged to remember what God had done in the past in what appeared to be hopeless situations.

'Look to the rock from which you were cut'. Remember the mighty deeds of the Lord. 'Look to Abraham, your father and to Sarah' mother of the nation. What a hopeless situation theirs was! Sarah was barren and well past childbearing age, yet God promised to raise their descendants into a great nation. God miraculously fulfilled his promise to them. In the same way God could be trusted to fulfil his promise to the faithful remnant to comfort them, to rebuild Jerusalem, and to restore the land of Israel. In fact, God's intention was to transform the desert places of the land to make them fruitful like the Garden of Eden. The present wastelands that had been ravished by the enemy and lay neglected and barren would soon blossom with new life and there would be joy and gladness there with 'thanksgiving and the sound of singing'.

Looking 'to the rock from which you were cut and the quarry from which you were hewn' means looking back on the path along which God has led you. Every believer in the Lord has past memories of times of blessing when God did something special, as he had done in the history of Israel. There are always times of depression or spiritual testing in every believer's life. It is at such times that we need to look back with thankfulness. It is good also to remember what God has done for others who put their trust in him, or to read the Bible with its multitude of stories of God's deliverance of his faithful servants. Even in the most difficult circumstances, or the darkest hour of the night, his promise that 'the Lord will surely comfort Zion' holds true for all who look to him. It is God's intention not only to comfort each believer, but to transform the whole of creation. Paul writes of this, 'The creation itself will be liberated from its bondage to decay and brought into the glorious freedom of the children of God' (Romans 8:21).

Prayer

Lord, deal with any sense of hopelessness or despair in my life. Replace it with hope and new life and joy.

JUSTICE OF RIGHTEOUSNESS

Isaiah 51: 4- 6

"Listen to me, my people; hear me, my nation: The law will go out from me; my justice will become a light to the nations. My righteousness draws near speedily, my salvation is on the way, and my arm will bring justice to the nations. The islands will look to me and wait in hope for my arm. Lift up your eyes to the heavens, look at the earth beneath; the heavens will vanish like smoke, the earth will wear out like a garment and its inhabitants die like flies. But my salvation will last forever, my righteousness will never fail.

Comment

God now speaks directly to his people, to the exiles in Babylon, to those who were open to listen to him. They are commanded to listen for an important announcement. The message is something of far greater significance than their release from Babylon. God speaks of the purpose he intends fulfilling through their return to the land of Israel and the spiritual renewal of the nation. 'The law will go out through me; my justice will become a light to the nations.' The bringing together here of Torah and justice is significant. 'Torah' is 'teaching' or 'instruction' and 'justice' is much more than our western concept of that word. In Hebraic thought justice was linked with relationships. The just man was in a right relationship with others and with God. This was worlds apart from the cold legalistic concept usually implied in western understanding.

The prophecy in this passage is that God will send out to all nations his teaching about right relationships which will bring light to all people. 'Righteousness' and 'justice' have the same root in Hebrew. The next statement in the prophecy is, 'My righteousness draws near speedily' and this is said to be God's salvation. Further understanding of what is being said here is given by the phrase 'my arm will bring justice to the nations.'

The arm of the Lord means his power. And all nations are said to be waiting for the power of the Lord to be displayed. This goes far beyond Israel and includes not only the neighbouring nations, but far off lands as well. The statement, 'The islands will look to me and wait in hope for my arm' means that even the distant nations to the ends of the earth will be looking and longing for God to come in power.

If we now put the three elements of this prophecy together we have **Torah, Justice and Power**. What is being referred to is clearly the reign of God, the messianic kingly reign, the establishment of the Kingdom of God on earth when Messiah will triumph over all the evil forces and the opponents of the Gospel. He will set the prisoners free and establish righteousness, right relationships, throughout the earth. Light and joy and freedom from oppression will come to all the nations! This is the salvation for which men of all nations will be longing. As the days get darker through the advancement of sin, violence, lawlessness, the breakdown of family, drugs, disease and all the evil of sinful humanity which brings untold suffering upon mankind, so people will long for the light, for God's light, the light of the world.

The great optimism of 19th century utopianism was shattered by 20th century bloodshed and moral anarchy. The deliberate cruelty of the Nazi European holocaust, the systematic murder of six million Jews, the slaughter of countless millions in war, the rise of mindless terrorism, the opulence of the rich and the poverty of the poor, the millions who die of hunger in a world of plenty, shows the extent of the injustice and inhumanity of man who trusts in material power and riches. But 'the earth will wear out like a garment, its inhabitants die like flies' because nothing is permanent - only the Kingdom of God, his salvation and his righteousness will last for ever and ever. The good news is that we don't have to wait to get into the Kingdom. Membership is open now! Citizenship is available immediately. The only qualification is trust in the Lord Jesus!

Prayer

Lord, help me not only to trust you myself, but to tell others the good news of your Kingdom, your kingly rule on earth.

THE FEAR OF MEN

Isaiah 51: 7- 8

"Hear me, you who know what is right, you people who have my law in your hearts: Do not fear the reproach of men or be terrified by their insults. For the moth will eat them up like a garment; the worm will devour them like wool. But my righteousness will last forever, my salvation through all generations."

Comment

This passage continues the theme of the preceding three verses. Isaiah was seeing the long-term purpose of God in renewing the nation of Israel and in the mission of the Servant of the Lord. He had spoken to the exiles of this, although it is doubtful if any of them understood what was being said to them. They could hardly have been expected to see beyond their own release from captivity and their dreams of returning to the land of Israel and being allowed to live in freedom.

Isaiah, however, was privileged to see beyond that, to God's purposes for all mankind. Here he envisages God's word going out far and wide so that the appeal was made to all 'who know what is right, you people who have my law in your hearts'. This is not just the people of Israel, but people of all nations who are truly seeking God, those who seek for truth - the God-fearers. They are exhorted not to fear 'the reproach of men, or be terrified by their insults'. This is a recognition that as soon as anyone accepts the Gospel, or receives the word of God, they are a target for the enemy. The parable Jesus told about the sower and the seed (Matthew 13) describes the attack upon the word of God in new believers. The seed on the pathway was immediately gobbled up by birds. The seed on rocky soil had no depth and had no roots to survive the heat of the day. The seed among thorns, Jesus said, was like 'a man who hears the word, but the worries of this life and the deceitfulness of wealth choke it, making it unfruitful' (Matthew 13:22).

This is a similar warning brought as a word from God by Isaiah. It is addressed to all who have the word of God in their hearts and is therefore timeless. We should expect opposition when we identify with the teaching of the Lord. His word is in direct opposition to the values of the world. The values of the Kingdom of God cannot mix with those of the world. It is like trying to mix oil and water. Isaiah was, of course, addressing the exiles in Babylon and exhorting them to be prepared to leave that city and go to Zion. He is here contrasting the two cities, Babylon and Zion, one represents the world, the other the city of God.

Those who elected to stay in Babylon would find their lives would be consumed by material and physical desires and consequences. They would end like a moth-eaten garment - fit for nothing but the scrap heap. The maggots of materialism and spiritual corruption would devour them. By contrast, those who embraced the word of God and were prepared to face 'the reproach of men' and not be afraid of their insults, would be held within the eternal embrace of the Father whose righteousness lasts for ever.

These are basic principles that last for all time. Those who reject the word of God and choose to go the way of the world put themselves outside the Kingdom of God. They never know the peace that is beyond human understanding, or the joy of knowing the closeness of the Lord. The warning in this passage is that we should never allow the fear of men to deter us from what we know is right. We should also be continually on watch for those who are struggling with such fear so that we can be alongside them to strengthen and to encourage them to stand firm in the strength of the Lord.

Prayer

Lord, help me to stand firm on your word and to use my witness to be a blessing to others.

EVERLASTING JOY

Isaiah 51: 9- 11

Awake, awake! Clothe yourself with strength, O arm of the Lord; awake, as in days gone by, as in generations of old. Was it not you who cut Rahab to pieces, who pierced that monster through? Was it not you who dried up the sea, the waters of the great deep, who made a road in the depths of the sea so that the redeemed might cross over? The ransomed of the Lord will return. They will enter Zion with singing; everlasting joy will crown their heads. Gladness and joy will overtake them, and sorrow and sighing will flee away.

Comment

This is almost word for word a community lament such as frequently occurs in the Psalms; eg Psalms 44, 74, 80, 83 and 85. It represents the heart cry of the captives in Babylon and may, in some measure, be a response to Isaiah's prophecies of the impending downfall of Babylon and the release of the exiles. We don't know how long Isaiah had been prophesying this and it is to be expected that these prophecies in chapters 40-55 will have been given over a period of perhaps several years.

Many of the exiles were, no doubt, getting impatient. When is God going to act to fulfil his promises? This lament looks back at the past in much the same way as Psalm 44. There, the Psalmist recalls the great things God had done in the past, but then says, 'But now you have rejected and humbled us' (v9) and then goes on to exhort, 'Awake, O Lord! Why do you sleep? Rouse yourself! Do not reject us for ever. Why do you hide your face and forget our misery and oppression?' (vv23-24). That Psalm bears clear marks of the exile in Babylon and it may well be what Isaiah is repeating here. So he calls for the power of God, 'O arm of the Lord' to be displayed as in days of old. The reference to 'Rahab ... that monster' is the cause of some division among commentators. Liberal theologians see here a reference to mythological creatures with whom the gods wrestled, such as Leviathan the monster of the sea referred to in Isaiah 27:1. Conservative theologians reject this on the grounds that Hebrew religion would have nothing to do with myths. They take the view that Rahab represents Egypt.

There are good grounds for interpreting this as Egypt, as in Isaiah 30:7. Egypt is called 'Rahab the do-nothing'. And there is a clear reference here to God drying out the waters of the Red Sea and making a path through the sea 'so that the redeemed might pass over'. The reference to Egypt is the most likely, but there is no reason why this should not have had a double meaning, as all the exiles would have been aware of the Babylonian myths. That does not mean that either they or Isaiah believed them! Indeed, they would see it as an affirmation of the all mighty power of the God of Israel.

Isaiah here was using the community lament to move into the joyous affirmation that God would soon act to set the people free to return to Zion with singing and with joy. He repeats almost word for word the prophecy of Isaiah 35:10, 'The ransomed of the Lord will return ... sorrow and sighing will flee away'. The hardest experience was that of the faithful remnant among the exiles. They did believe the prophecy. They were convinced that God would answer their prayers and that he would hear their cries. But why was he waiting so long? Could he not step in NOW, as he had done in times past, and bare his arm of power?

It is always the faithful ones who suffer most. The unbelievers, who have made friends with the world, are not looking to God. He is of no account to them. But faithful believers long to see God fulfilling his promises. Sometimes the hardest thing to accept is God's slowness in acting. We often have to wait years to see him fulfil a promise and sometimes it even runs over to another generation. God's timing is not ours, but he is faithful and all his promises will be fulfilled. The day will come when we will join with God's released captives of the centuries and all God's faithful ones and everlasting joy will crown our heads.

Prayer
Hasten the day, O Lord, when you fulfil your promises to your people.

COVERED BY THE LORD

Isaiah 51: 12- 14,16
**I, even I, am he who comforts you. Who are you that you
fear mortal men, the sons of men, who are but grass, that
you forget the Lord your Maker, who stretched out the
heavens and laid the foundations of the earth, that you live
in constant terror every day because of the wrath of the
oppressor, who is bent on destruction? The cowering
prisoners will soon be set free; they will not die in their
dungeon, nor will they lack bread. I have put my words in
your mouth and covered you with the shadow of my hand –
I who set the heavens in place, who laid the foundations of
the earth, and who say to Zion, 'You are my people.'**

Comment

This is God's answer to the community lament in vv 9-11. The
lament was an implied complaint against God, saying that he
had done great things of old, why did he not do them now?
God's answer in these verses is a complaint against his people. It
begins with the emphatic, 'I, even I AM' and goes straight to the
reminder that he is the one who comforts, that is, strengthens,
rescues and redeems his people.

God's complaint against his people is, 'Who are you that fear
mortal men, the sons of men who are but grass?' He says, 'You
live in constant terror every day because of the wrath of the
oppressor'. This really meant that the oppressor had become
more important than God. The exiles were so aware of their
masters that they had forgotten God.

Their oppressors were there in front of them, larger than life,
whereas God was unseen. They had forgotten that the
oppressors were only mortal men and by their attitude they had
elevated them to gods. In effect, they were bowing down before
them. The oppressors were exercising a controlling spirit that was
dominating the lives of the people of God and making them

forget the almighty power of God.

It is easy for us to criticise the exiles in Babylon for their fear of their taskmasters, but whenever we allow someone to exercise control over our lives we are doing the same thing and we are not putting God first. Of course, we may have to work under discipline at our place of work and similarly in our Christian service, if we are part of a Christian community, we respect the authority of eldership. But this does not mean that we allow anyone to exercise spiritual control over us. We are accountable to God, not to mortal man and while we respect elders and listen to the counsel of others, we are not to be dominated by fear. To do so is to 'forget the Lord your Maker who stretched out the heavens and laid the foundations of the earth'.

There is really no excuse for living 'in constant terror every day because of the wrath of the oppressor'. Even under extreme circumstances of oppression it is possible for believers to focus upon God in such a way that the oppressor cannot dominate our spirit.

The story of Corrie Ten Boom, the Dutch believer, who was sent to a Nazi concentration camp for sheltering Jewish people who were being sent to the gas chambers, is an example of the triumph of love. She and her sister suffered terrible treatment from their evil oppressors, but they refused to let hatred dominate them, or bitterness blight their souls. They continually focused upon the love of God and his power to overcome evil. The oppressors were only mortal men, who 'are but grass'.

God's promise to his people is the same as he gave to the Servant-Redeemer in the last verse of this passage, 'I have put my words in your mouth and covered you with the shadow of my hand'. It is his covering that gives us protection of mind and spirit against all that evil oppressors can do. He is the one who set the heavens in place and 'laid the foundations of the earth' who says to all believers in the Lord Jesus, 'You are my people'.

Prayer

Set your cover over me, O Lord, that I may focus my mind upon you.

AWAKE, AWAKE!

Isaiah 51: 17- 20

Awake, awake! Rise up, O Jerusalem, you who have drunk from the hand of the Lord the cup of his wrath, you who have drained to its dregs the goblet that makes men stagger. Of all the sons she bore there was none to guide her; of all the sons she brought up there was none to take her by the hand. These double calamities have come upon you – who can comfort you? – ruin and destruction, famine and sword – who can console you? Your sons have fainted; they lie at the head of every street, like antelope caught in a net. They are filled with the wrath of the Lord and the rebuke of your God.

Comment

This is another community lament but, although the language is similar to that of 51:9 which also begins, 'Awake! Awake!', the speaker here is God, in contrast to 51:9 where it is the exiles who are calling upon God to awake. Here it is God calling upon Jerusalem to awake and arise out of her drunken stupor.

These verses take up the lament of the people in terms very similar to those of Lamentations where vivid descriptions are given of the terrible destruction of Jerusalem and the violence done to her people by the Babylonians. In Lamentations there is no mention of Babylon. It is the Lord who is blamed for all the terrible things that happened to Jerusalem; 'Without pity the Lord has swallowed up all the dwellings of Jacob' (2:2). 'The Lord is like an enemy who has swallowed up Israel' (2:5). 'He has laid waste his dwelling like a garden; he has destroyed his place of meeting' (2:6). 'The Lord determined to tear down the wall around the Daughter of Zion. ... Her gates have sunk into the ground; their bars he has broken and destroyed' (2:8-9).

It is this kind of direct complaint against God that here he throws back at them by repeating some of these complaints to show that he is not deaf to their cries. He has heard and he is acting now to redeem them. But the spiritual message God wishes to get home to them is that the real tragedy is that they are not learning the lessons of the destruction of Jerusalem. Instead of saying, 'Why did God allow it?' they are reeling like a drunken old woman with no-one to take her by the hand and lead her home.

Yes, Jerusalem has suffered greatly, double calamity; ruin and destruction have come upon the land, and famine and sword have afflicted the people. There is no-one to console Zion. She is like a widow who has lost all her sons and has been forced to drink a potent goblet and is now staggering drunkenly through the ruins of the city, seeking refuge, but there is no strong hand to take her and guide her to safety. It is a vivid picture and one that arouses great compassion for the shattered citizens of a once proud and great city. The answer to the lament is given in the next section, the final verses of this chapter. But here the message is that God has fully heard the complaints of his people and he is dealing with the situation.

Before he tells them what he intends doing, God rebukes his people for continuing to wallow in their misery. These images of ruin and destruction had occurred nearly fifty years earlier. Isaiah was prophesying just a few years before the conquest of Babylon in 539 BC, Jerusalem had fallen in 586 BC, and here the people were still filled with the images of destruction which were destroying their peace. God wanted to see his people turn from the misery of failure to the new hope of faith. It was faith in God which was now required. God sometimes has to speak sharply to us to tell us to stop dwelling in the past and being dominated by past tragedies or failures, but to let faith arise. He tells us to trust him and he will bring us to a place of victory and turn our mourning into joy.

Prayer

Lord, show me if there are areas of my life that I need to leave behind and to trust you for the future.

GOD DEFENDS HIS PEOPLE

Isaiah 51: 21- 23
Therefore hear this, you afflicted one, made drunk, but not with wine. This is what your Sovereign Lord says, your God, who defends his people: "See, I have taken out of your hand the cup that made you stagger; from that cup, the goblet of my wrath, you will never drink again. I will put it into the hands of your tormentors, who said to you, 'Fall prostrate that we may walk over you.' And you made your back like the ground, like a street to be walked over."

Comment

The problem with Judah, after many years in exile, was that the people were defeated in spirit as well as physically. They had lost all self-respect. Again, we turn to Lamentations for a word picture of the condition of the exiles, 'Look, O Lord, and consider, for I am despised. Is it nothing to you, all you who pass by? Look around and see. Is any suffering like my suffering?' (1:11-12). 'No-one is near to comfort me, no-one to restore my spirit' (1:16).

When a people feel of no self-worth it is as difficult to help them as it is with those who are completely the opposite - full of self-importance! A total lack of self-esteem means that a person is not open to help, their spirit is so depressed that they are ground down by despair. This was the condition of many of the exiles, and in order to help them God had to give the sharp wake-up call in v17. He had to get them to raise their heads sufficiently to hear what he had to say. Yes, they had been badly humiliated. Their oppressors had walked all over them. Their tormentors had said, 'Fall prostrate so that we may walk over you'. This was not uncommon as a means of humiliation. Joshua did it to some kings he captured. He made his army commanders come and stand on them (Joshua 10:24). But Israel needed to look to the reason why God had allowed them to be humiliated. Once the people were ready to repent, then they would be open to God's healing and comfort. He could then work the transformation of their physical condition. He first had to change their mind set, their mental attitude, and this was dependent upon their spiritual health.

Once Israel was prepared to face up to the fact that she had not trusted the Lord, but had played the harlot with idols and run after foreign gods and trusted in pacts and treaties with other nations and not put her trust in the Lord - then her whole attitude would change and she would be open to receiving the blessing God was longing to pour into her.

Israel had indeed drunk deeply from the cup of wrath. Jeremiah had spent his entire ministry of more than forty years warning of the tragedy that would befall the nation. He was told on one occasion to take a cup of wine, representing the wrath of the Lord, and make all the nations drink from it, beginning with Jerusalem, and all the towns of Judah (Jeremiah 25:15f). God's promise now was one of complete healing. He was going to reverse the situation. Those nations he had used to humble his own people would now drink from the same cup. Those nations who had gone much farther in cruelty than the Lord had wanted would now receive the just penalty of their wickedness.

This was the promise of 'the God who defends his people' who was not only their God, but also Israel's 'husband' - this is a better translation than the term 'Sovereign Lord' (NIV). God was saying to Jerusalem, who felt herself to be widowed, that he was still her husband, who cared for her and would defend her and redeem her, as Hosea had done for his errant wife.

God longs to raise up those who feel downcast and depressed. He speaks into that situation and drives away the spirit of darkness and depression saying, 'I am your defender, your kinsman-redeemer, and I love you and I will never let you go.'

Prayer
Lord, let the light of your love reach into the dark places of my life that I keep hidden, even from myself!

TAKE OFF THE CHAINS

Isaiah 52: 1- 3

Awake, awake, O Zion, clothe yourself with strength. Put on your garments of splendour, O Jerusalem, the holy city. The uncircumcised and defiled will not enter you again. Shake off your dust; rise up, sit enthroned, O Jerusalem. Free yourself from the chains on your neck, O captive Daughter of Zion. For this is what the Lord says: "You were sold for nothing, and without money you will be redeemed."

Comment

This passage contains the theme of messages between God and the exiles begun in chapter 51. There is a deliberate repetition here of the words found in 51:9. The difference is in the speaker. In 51:9 the people were crying out to God to awake and come to their rescue. Here it is God calling upon his people to awake and put on strength. This may seem strange, since they are captives and have no strength to free themselves. But God was trying to shake them out of their attitude of apathy and despair that characterised them as a defeated people. The call was to a renewal of hope through faith in God. They had to remove the garments of mourning and put on beautiful clothes as befitted the people of God.

The message was a declaration of God's intention to protect Jerusalem once it was restored. 'The uncircumcised and defiled will not enter you again'. This did not only mean foreign armies would not again ravish the land, but that the uncircumcised of Israel would also be banned. God was proclaiming Jerusalem as a holy city, and setting it apart for his glory. The law would go out from Zion, this was the prophecy of Isaiah 2, that in the messianic age the word of God would go out from Jerusalem to all parts of the world. This prophecy foreshadowed that great messianic event. It said that God was rebuilding Jerusalem for that very purpose. It was now time to begin to act on this promise, to show faith in their God, that he would fulfil his promise.

Jerusalem was to be a holy city for all the world to see her majesty. So the people should begin to reflect the glory of God NOW. It was time to shake off the dust of mourning and to hold their heads high as befits those who are citizens of God's city. The command, 'Free yourself from the chains on your neck, O captive Daughter of Zion' is not a cruel jest. God had already broken the chains of captivity in the spiritual realm, the physical would soon follow. Therein lies a basic spiritual principle.

The people had to experience a radical change of attitude. God had already set them free, but they had to claim it by moving into the realm of spiritual freedom from oppression. There are things that only God can do, but there are also things that we have to do for ourselves. Only Jesus had the power to raise Lazarus from the dead. But he did not remove the grave-clothes. He ordered others to do that! (John 11:44). God will not do for us what we must do for ourselves!

God reminded the exiles that they were 'sold for nothing' he did not have to sell them because he was bankrupt. He allowed the enemy to triumph because of his people's sin. He would redeem them himself, at no cost to them, because they could not do this for themselves.

Only God can give new life. Only he can transform a situation from despair and disaster into new life and hope. We have to shake off the grave-clothes, the attitude of despair, and put on the garment of faith and praise. The Lord looks to see the rising faith of his people as they embrace the reality of new life in Christ.

Prayer
Thank you, Lord, that you have broken the chains. Help me to throw off anything that hampers the word of your Holy Spirit.

YOUR GOD REIGNS!

Isaiah 52: 7- 9

How beautiful on the mountains are the feet of those who bring good news, who proclaim peace, who bring good tidings, who proclaim salvation, who say to Zion, "Your God reigns!" Listen! Your watchmen lift up their voices; together they shout for joy. When the Lord returns to Zion, they will see it with their own eyes. Burst into songs of joy together, you ruins of Jerusalem, for the Lord has comforted his people, he has redeemed Jerusalem.

Comment

This is a wonderful piece of prophetic poetry, probably originally a song, a prophetic song sung by the prophet caught up in the Spirit! In order to get the full flavour of what was being conveyed to the people in exile in Babylon awaiting their release to return to Jerusalem, it is necessary to use a little imagination. Isaiah had been foretelling the downfall of Babylon and preparing the people for their release and return to the land of Israel. Now, with this poem, he reached the summit of revelation as he saw the fulfilment of the promises of God.

Isaiah saw this in the picture of a city in a land occupied by the enemy. The citizens were aware that a decisive battle was taking place elsewhere that would determine their fate. If there was victory they would be spared and liberated from the fear of death. But if there was a defeat it would seal their own doom. The kind of picture Isaiah was seeing was that of a watchman on the wall who sees a runner in the far distance. A messenger is coming with news of the battle, but is it good news or bad? As he draws nearer he can be seen waving his arms in jubilation. In fact, he is dancing as well as running! His feet are already proclaiming the message that his mouth will soon declare. How beautiful are his feet! Soon the watchman alerts the other watchmen on the walls around the city. They begin to shout in unison.

'Listen! Your watchmen lift up their voices; together they shout for joy'. This is how it will be when the Lord returns to Zion. All the people will hear the good news of the messenger and will join their voices to swell the chorus of the watchmen. The whole city will 'burst into songs of joy. When the Lord returns to Zion, they will see it with their own eyes'. The ruins of Jerusalem and the waste places of the land will join in the great chorus of praise to the God who has demonstrated his faithfulness to his people and his power to all the world.

Once again we see here the power of prophetic revelation. The prophet sees, as accomplished reality, that which has not yet happened. It is revealed to him so vividly by God, and his confidence in the Lord is so great, that he sees it and is able to declare it as a finished work. It is seeing things in the spiritual realm that have yet to take place in the physical - that is genuine prophecy!

This is one of the outstanding examples of prophecy in the Bible. Isaiah was shown what actually happened a few years later. He saw it in its spiritual significance, not just as the return of weary, dirt-covered, liberated slaves coming back to a ruined city. He saw it as the triumphant return of the Lord to the holy city from which his word would one day go out to all nations. He saw also a glimpse of the eternal heavenly city of God and the coming reign of God in the messianic age. Perhaps, like John on the island of Patmos centuries later, he saw it coming down out of heaven in all its glory and majesty. 'For the Lord has comforted his people, he has redeemed Jerusalem' he proclaimed.

It is still a message on the lips of all true believers who by faith know that, although we live in a land surrounded by the enemy, our God will be seen by all the world to be victorious. In the spiritual realm God has already won the victory and we can proclaim with confidence, 'Our God reigns!'

Prayer

Lord, we are lost for words to praise you. We are so thankful that you reign in this fallen world.

DEPART, DEPART!

Isaiah 52: 10- 12

The Lord will lay bare his holy arm in the sight of all the nations, and all the ends of the earth will see the salvation of our God. Depart, depart, go out from there! Touch no unclean thing! Come out from it and be pure, you who carry the vessels of the Lord. But you will not leave in haste or go in flight; for the Lord will go before you, the God of Israel will be your rear guard.

Comment

At last we reach the climax of the message begun in chapter 40, where the proclamation of comfort to Israel was declared. The climax now comes with the command to, 'Depart, depart!' But, before that long-awaited command was issued, there is a link verse providing a bridge between the glorious good news of the reign of God and the instruction to the exiles to leave Babylon. 'The Lord will lay bare his holy arm in the sight of all nations'. The thing that God intends doing in redeeming Israel and rebuilding Jerusalem as the holy city, has significance for all the world. If God is truly the only God, Creator of the universe and Lord of all nations, then the good news of his reign is for all nations, not just for Israel. Indeed, what benefits Israel is for the benefit of all the world, since Israel is the chosen servant of the Lord through whom he will reveal his salvation to all peoples. Thus, 'the ends of the earth will see the salvation of our God'.

Just as God's salvation goes far beyond Israel, so too does the command, 'Depart, depart, go out from there!' The clue to understanding the wider spiritual significance in these words lies in the next words, 'Touch no unclean thing! Come out from it and be pure'. Certainly these words, in the first instance, were addressed to the exiles as they anticipated the exodus from Babylon. This would not be in haste, as was the departure of their forefathers from Egypt, when they didn't even have time for the yeast to rise in their bread. Their withdrawal from Babylon would be orderly and well organised, not a hasty flight. They would take with them the holy vessels from the temple plundered by Nebuchadnezzar. The Lord would go before them, preparing the way, and would be their rear-guard as he went before and behind the people of Israel at the Exodus from Egypt - a cloud by day and a pillar of fire by night.

The faithful remnant among the exiles would respond immediately to the call to leave Babylon, but there would be waverers, those who saw the opportunity of making a lucrative living in the city that had once been the place of their oppression. No doubt some would be tempted to stay rather than to make the long, arduous journey by foot back to Judah. This is an exhortation to all those who value the word of God, and who recognise that it is God who has liberated them and given them the offer of new life, to enter fully into that new life. The attractions of the world are always there and they especially appeal to those who are not fully committed to God.

The battle for pre-eminence between Babylon and Jerusalem has already lasted for thousands of years and is likely to last for some time to come. It will last until Messiah comes again and establishes his reign of love and justice on the earth. Until that time the material riches of Babylon will continue to ensnare many. Despite the warnings of the Lord to 'Come out from it and be pure' the temptation of 'Mammon' will lure many away from the truth. It is so easy to fall into the traps of self-indulgence. Money, sex, and power adopt various guises to bewitch the unwary. The only sure way of avoiding falling into the pit is to be fully committed to the word of God, constantly studying it, so that the reality of the living God grows day by day. The values of the Kingdom then become part of our very being and we long for the day when 'the ends of the earth will see the salvation of our God' and Babylon will be destroyed for ever!

Prayer
Hasten that day, O Lord, and in the meantime use me to spread the good news of your Kingdom.

HIGHLY EXALTED

Isaiah 52: 13- 15

See, my servant will act wisely; he will be raised and lifted up and highly exalted. Just as there were many who were appalled at him – his appearance was so disfigured beyond that of any man and his form marred beyond human likeness – so will he sprinkle many nations, and kings will shut their mouths because of him. For what they were not told, they will see, and what they have not heard, they will understand.

Comment

This is the fourth and final Servant Song. It begins in the same way as the first song in 42:1, 'Behold, my servant' (AV). This is not merely an introduction, but it is meant to be an indication of an important announcement. The Servant has a special mission which is about to be described and it is necessary to pay careful attention to what is being said. The Servant is going to be 'raised and lifted up and highly exalted'. His status is going to be high throughout the world. This section is God's commendation of his servant. The next three sections describe the Servant's humiliation and suffering; while the final section, 53:10-12, returns to the voice of God speaking about his Servant.

The theme that is worked out through these sections is the way in which God is going to overcome sin. It will not be through a display of the power of God, the arm of the Lord. On the contrary, it will be by allowing the Servant to be crushed by the enemy and then being raised up. He will take upon himself the sin of his people Israel and of the Gentile nations in a similar manner to that of the scapegoat in the sacrificial system of Israel (Leviticus 16:10 and 21-22).

The NIV translation 'my servant will act wisely' is somewhat misleading. A better rendering is 'my servant will prosper'. He will have the wisdom and knowledge to accomplish his purpose.

He will therefore be raised up and highly exalted. Many will be appalled at the suffering of the servant. He will be subjected to terrible injuries so that his appearance is disfigured and his body injured. This will startle, or astonish, the nations. The word translated 'sprinkle' in the NIV is clearly wrong. The Hebrew consonants can be translated 'sprinkle' or 'startle'. The Septuagint LXX (Greek version) has 'many nations will marvel at him'. This meaning is the only one that makes sense. What is here being said is that, just as many were appalled at his suffering, so they will be astonished at his exaltation. The humiliation of the Servant of God will astound the world, but the nations will be even more startled, amazed, and astounded at his exaltation through the world. In fact world rulers, kings, 'will shut their mouths because of him', they will be speechless. If they had not seen it with their own eyes they would not believe it. The One who was utterly defeated comes back to life and becomes the most celebrated One in the world. The rulers are startled, it is almost unbelievable!

This is God's method of dealing with sin. It is entirely different from anything the world could devise. It does not fit into our concept of justice. Why should the innocent suffer for the guilty? But this is God's way of redemption. Paul says we have been bought with a price (1 Corinthians 6:20). He emphasises that God has done for us what we were powerless to do for ourselves, that is, to break the grip that sin has upon our lives which holds us enslaved. He says, 'God demonstrated his own love for us in this; while we were still sinners, Christ died for us' (Romans 5:8).

God's ways are not our ways, but the way of salvation he chose was to allow his Servant, the Messiah, to suffer and to die so that in his risen power all may have new life. No wonder the rulers of the world are speechless when they see that love is a greater power than all their armies with their weapons of mass destruction. The love of God triumphs over all evil.

Prayer

Thank you, Father, that you so loved the world as to send your Son.

DESPISED AND REJECTED

Isaiah 53: 1- 3

Who has believed our message and to whom has the arm of the Lord been revealed? He grew up before him like a tender shoot, and like a root out of dry ground. He had no beauty or majesty to attract us to him, nothing in his appearance that we should desire him. He was despised and rejected by men, a man of sorrows, and familiar with suffering. Like one from whom men hide their faces he was despised, and we esteemed him not.

Comment

'Who has believed our message'. It is not clear who the speaker is. Those who believe Israel is the Servant will say that the speaker is the Gentile nations reporting on the suffering of Israel. Those who believe the Servant is the Messiah will say that the speaker is either Israel or the prophets of Israel.

Clearly there is astonishment, both in Israel and among the nations, that the arm of the Lord has been bared, as he promised, to redeem his people. When his arm was seen it was not as anyone had expected. In the physical realm he had done nothing spectacular to release his people from captivity; he had used Cyrus to break the power of Babylon. The return of the exiles to Jerusalem had been unspectacular and the renewal of the nation had not made them a great high-status international power. But that was not God's way! God does not do things the world's way. The Servant was not an attractive, charismatic leader, drawing people to follow him by the magnetism of his personality and his exercise of impressive superhuman power and glory. That is the world's way. It is not God's way.

It was God's intention to allow the Servant to suffer and to be humiliated. Paul beautifully expresses this in Philippians 2:6-11. He says that Jesus, the Messiah, 'made himself nothing, taking the very nature of a servant ... he humbled himself and became obedient to death - even death on a cross! Therefore God exalted him to the highest place and gave him a name that is above every name'.

In order to understand this section, it must be seen in the context of the whole of chapters 40-53. God's intention was to renew Israel; to bring about a spiritual transformation of the nation, as his chosen vessel for conveying his word to the world. The Servant Songs were to show the true nature of the servanthood for which God was looking.

The world thinks of leadership in terms of dominant personalities, whereas God was wanting to reach the nations through love and self-sacrifice. The Servant whom God sent to the world 'had no beauty or majesty'. In fact, right from the start, his entry into the world was unspectacular. 'He grew up before him like a tender shoot'. He could so easily have been snuffed out, like a careless gardener might snip off a tender shoot that should grow into a fine plant.

Sending the Messiah in this way was an enormous risk, but that was God's way. He sent his Messiah, born to a humble girl in a backyard stable, not in a palace. He grew up in a statusless village among humble working people. When he did come among the rich and the powerful, 'He was despised and rejected by men'. His end was one of deepest humiliation, nailed virtually naked to a cross, for all the public to see and to mock. But that was God's way of redeeming Israel.

The world would have done it in a different way. But who can understand God's ways? His thoughts are not ours and in this passage we reach the climax of the contrast between Babylon and Zion, between the ways of the world and God's ways, between the values of Mammon and the values of the Kingdom of God. Like Joshua, we are faced with a choice, 'Choose for yourselves this day whom you will serve' (Joshua 24:15).

Prayer
Lord, help me to respond as Joshua did, 'As for me and my household, we will serve the Lord!'

ALL WE LIKE SHEEP

Isaiah 53: 4- 6
Surely he took up our infirmities and carried our sorrows, yet we considered him stricken by God, smitten by him, and afflicted. But he was pierced for our transgressions, he was crushed for our iniquities; the punishment that brought us peace was upon him, and by his wounds we are healed. We all, like sheep, have gone astray, each of us has turned to his own way; and the Lord has laid on him the iniquity of us all.

Comment

The beautiful poetry of this passage moves from the description in vv1-3 of one who was disfigured and despised and rejected to the discovery that his sufferings were somehow connected with us. The 'report' expresses amazement at this discovery that is totally at variance with conventional thinking. In the thought of the day all suffering was a punishment for sin. All religions concurred with this. The one who suffered had somehow offended the gods and was experiencing the consequences. This is the theme of the book of Job. Job's friends were in no doubt that all the mishaps that had befallen him were thoroughly deserved. Hence Job's dilemma and his protestations of righteousness.

The awful realisation that this man, whom they had despised for the suffering he was enduring was, in fact, pierced for their transgressions, was a terrible shock. Such statements as 'the punishment that brought us peace was upon him, and by his wounds we are healed' can only be understood in light of the Hebrew sacrificial system.

Hebrews 9:22, reflecting Leviticus 17:11, says, 'Without the shedding of blood there is no forgiveness'. But the prophet Micah questioned the effectiveness of using the sacrificial death of an animal to atone for the sins of a human being. He concluded that what God really required was 'to act justly and to love mercy and to walk humbly with your God' (Micah 6:8).

Other prophets expressed similar reservations about the sacrificial system that made no heart-changes in the individual sinners; eg Isaiah 1:11, Jeremiah 6:20, Amos 5:22. But here something different is being said. To the amazement of the speakers, they discover that the suffering of the servant brings them 'shalom', that is peace, well-being and wholeness. This can only mean reconciliation with God - being in a right relationship with God.

'By his wounds we are healed'. That was the mystery. And it still is a mystery how God achieves our reconciliation, because we all know that we are sinners and that sin separates us from a holy God. Our sinfulness acts as a barrier to fellowship with God. But God himself has taken the initiative. He knows that 'We all, like sheep, have gone astray' and he alone knows the full consequences in eternity of our sin cutting us off from eternal life and from God. This is the central message of the gospel. We are all in danger of going to a lost-eternity. If God had not intervened to break the powers of death that would have been our fate. But when we accept Jesus as Saviour he opens up a new and living way.

God's way of bringing us back to himself, into a close and loving relationship, was by using his servant, the Messiah, who willingly took our sinfulness upon himself so that we should be set free. He broke the chains of our enslavement. 'The Lord has laid on him the iniquity of us all'. 'God was reconciling the world to himself in Christ' (2 Corinthians 5:19).

Prayer

Father, even if I cannot understand the mystery of reconciliation, help me to receive new life in Christ.

LIKE A LAMB

Isaiah 53: 7- 9

He was oppressed and afflicted, yet he did not open his mouth; he was led like a lamb to the slaughter, and as a sheep before her shearers is silent, so he did not open his mouth. By oppression and judgment he was taken away. And who can speak of his descendants? For he was cut off from the land of the living; for the transgression of my people he was stricken. He was assigned a grave with the wicked, and with the rich in his death, though he had done no violence, nor was any deceit in his mouth.

Comment

If there was any doubt about the identity of the servant, was it the nation Israel or an individual, these verses settle it. Quite clearly an individual is spoken of here. The opening phrases pick up on the closing lines of the preceding verse which used the simile of sheep going astray. Now in these verses it is not the people, but the Servant, who is like a sheep but the contrast could not be greater.

The people equate to the negative characteristics of sheep - their tendency to wander off thoughtlessly. But the Servant is identified with the positive characteristics of the gentle patience of sheep and the lovely innocence of a lamb, who so trusts the shepherd that he goes without protest to be slaughtered. The sheep also makes no sound when in the hands of the shearer.

It is 'by oppression and judgment' that the Servant was led away. It was a travesty of justice that condemned him to death. But, just as we were concluding that it was the wickedness of an unjust system that oppressed an innocent victim, the brilliance of this prophetic poem swings our focus around to ourselves! The speaker suddenly announces that it was 'for the transgressions of my people he was stricken'. It is not clear who the speaker is, therefore who 'my people' are. Clearly the speaker is not God, but the context does not necessarily mean the nation Israel. The best explanation appears to be that the anonymous speaker is speaking on behalf of the people of the world, sinful human beings, who discover that the Servant has died for them.

The phrases 'who can speak of his descendants?' and 'he was cut off from the land of the living' refer to the Servant dying childless. In the ancient Middle East this was considered a tragedy. The book of Ruth is an illustration of how important it was to Naomi to have an heir to bear the family name. In fact, popular belief was that survival somehow depended on the family name being continued in their heirs. Those who were unable to have children were considered cursed by God. Hence the amazement of the people who considered that the Servant was cursed by God, and then discovered that he had been stricken for others. Most importantly, he was not merely the innocent victim of injustice; he willingly sacrificed himself. Even though he was totally innocent he was 'assigned a grave with the wicked'. This indicated that the significance of his death was not recognised at the time. Just as no-one, not even the disciples, recognised the significance of Jesus' death until later.

It is not difficult to see the connection between the Servant in this passage and the crucifixion of the Lord Jesus. In the Gospel record we have the account of his unjust trial with false witnesses, dying in a manner apparently cursed by God, and being crucified alongside criminals. He was even laid to rest in a rich man's grave. But, of course, we have to go beyond the crucifixion to the resurrection of Jesus to understand the full meaning of his death. But that is not foretold in these verses of Isaiah.

Prayer
Lord, increase my understanding of your death for sinners like me.

THE LIGHT OF LIFE

Isaiah 53: 10-12
Yet it was the Lord's will to crush him and cause him to suffer, and though the Lord makes his life a guilt offering, he will see his offspring and prolong his days, and the will of the Lord will prosper in his hand. After the suffering of his soul, he will see the light of life and be satisfied; by his knowledge my righteous servant will justify many, and he will bear their iniquities. Therefore I will give him a portion among the great, and he will divide the spoils with the strong, because he poured out his life unto death, and was numbered with the transgressors. For he bore the sin of many, and made intercession for the transgressors.

Comment

We now come to the climax of the Servant Songs and to the conclusion to be drawn from all the foregoing prophetic poetry. God himself takes centre stage in these final verses, making it clear that the suffering and death of his Servant was no accident. It was not the outcome of an unjust human system or due to the powerlessness of a righteous man to stand against the wickedness and violence of humanity. Quite the contrary, it was God's will that the Servant should suffer. There was divine purpose in each part of what happened to the Servant. He was, in fact, a 'guilt offering'. Many years later John the Baptist was to say of Jesus, when he came for baptism at the Jordan, 'Behold the Lamb of God who takes away the sin of the world!' (John 1:29).

People had thought that the Servant who died childless and in circumstances of extreme suffering and humiliation was cursed by God. They thought his name was cut off from the land of the living. But God reverses all that and says that, far from being childless, the Servant 'will see his offspring and prolong his days, and the will of the Lord will prosper in his hands'. He will have children of many nations. His family will go on increasing across the world until the end of time, because God has chosen to work out his purposes through his Servant, therefore the 'will of the Lord will prosper'.

Verses 1 and 2 present many difficulties of translation, but the general theme of the Hebrew text presents the suffering of the Servant as a deliberate choice of God through which he, the Servant, would see the 'light of life' and be raised to new life. Through knowledge of him many will be justified, that is, made righteous. Their ability to be in a right relationship with God will be an outcome of the Servant having borne their iniquities. God's own testimony at the conclusion reaffirms the opening statement at the beginning of this Servant Song (52:13) that the Servant will be 'lifted up and highly exalted'. Because of what he has done in pouring out his life unto death, God 'will give him a portion among the great'. His inheritance will be among the greatest in world history and his followers will be the most numerous. This seems a better translation than 'he will divide the spoils with the strong'.

The final words, 'For he bore the sin of many and made intercession for the transgressors' can surely only be applied to Jesus, who in his death prayed for those who condemned him and those who nailed him to the cross. 'Father, forgive them, for they do not know what they are doing' (Luke 23:34). Even in the extremities of pain, Jesus still thought of others and he promised the thief dying on a cross alongside him a place with him in paradise (Luke 23:43). The victorious sacrifice of Jesus for our sins can never be fully comprehended by our finite human minds. But the witness of the Spirit within each believer bears testimony to the new life we enter the moment we accept that Jesus has done for us something that we could not do for ourselves. Our sins are forgiven and we are brought into a new relationship with God the Father through the Son, our Saviour, who is indeed the 'light of life'.

Prayer
Father, through the ongoing ministry of your Holy Spirit, bring many to know the light of life in Jesus. Thank you for the privilege of being part of the family of your righteous Servant.

INDEX OF HEADINGS

INDEX OF READINGS

In the same series:

Today With Jeremiah Volume I

Available from Christian Bookshops and The Centre for Biblical and Hebraic Studies, The Park, Moggerhanger, Bedford, MK44 3RW, UK. Price £6.00 + £1.00 UK postage – ISBN: 1-872395-55-4

This is a new approach to understanding the message of the prophet Jeremiah. Dr Hill has spent many years studying the prophets. He sees special relevance in the life and work of Jeremiah for today.

This is a series of daily readings in Jeremiah covering the first half of the book. Each reading has an explanation of the message with an application for today. If you really want to understand the message of Jeremiah for today this book will provide you with a feast that you will want to read and reread.

'*Today with Jeremiah* provides a daily commentary on the book of Jeremiah, explaining both the background and the meaning. Each day the devotional challenge and application is highly relevant. I warmly commend it.' *Viscount Brentford*

'Here in an accessible format for every concerned Christian is a clear exposition of the main features of Jeremiah's teaching. In plain terms, these pages help us understand the message and apply it to today's world.' *David Anderson (from the Foreword)*

In the same series:

Today With Isaiah Volume 1

Available from Christian Bookshops and The Centre for Biblical and Hebraic Studies, The Park, Moggerhanger, Bedford, MK44 3RW, UK. Price £6.00 + £1.00 UK postage – ISBN: 1-872395-60-0

The book of Isaiah is, by any standard, a treasure trove of spiritual riches. In the Hebrew Bible it is given the foremost place in the section known as 'The Latter Prophets'.

There is great consistency in Isaiah's message, which was set against the background of international politics and dominated by the constant threat from Assyria. Throughout his long ministry, Isaiah stood firmly against immorality, injustice, oppression and idolatry.

In order to understand the message, it is necessary to know the background, the culture and the idioms of the day in which the word of God was conveyed to the people. When these are unravelled, the spiritual gems are revealed.

In Volume 1 of Today with Isaiah, Dr Hill uses sensitivity and scholarship to open up the background to the text of Isaiah and to provide a fresh spiritual message day by day.

The *Revd John Fieldsend*, himself a Messianic Jew, writes *'No-one is in a better position to relate Isaiah's message to our daily lives than Clifford Hill. This book will enrich the lives of all who seek a renewal and enlargement of faith, by allowing Isaiah to speak anew into the daily experiences of personal life.'* (from the Foreword)

In the same series:

Today With Jeremiah Volume 2

Available from Christian Bookshops and The Centre for Biblical and Hebraic Studies, The Park, Moggerhanger, Bedford, MK44 3RW, UK. Price £6.00 + £1.00 UK postage – ISBN: 1-872395-65-1

Jeremiah was one of the greatest prophets of ancient Israel – a man who was a keen observer of the world around him. There are many similarities between our present world situation and the times in which Jeremiah lived. This gives added relevance to the study of the message of this remarkable man of God.

In this devotional commentary Dr Clifford Hill brings the message alive in a way that is both fresh and challenging, yet always readable and never dull.

In the Foreword to this volume Dr Denton writes 'Here then is the second volume, completing the daily readings from Jeremiah, presented in a way that will stand the test of academic rigour, while conveying the heart of God for our times in a relevant way. You will find your heart warmed and softened as you study.'

'To many, Jeremiah is the most human of all the prophets. He exposes his angst and frustrations about his ministry in a way that is rare amongst the other mouthpieces of God. Any serious commentary on his prophecies, therefore, must integrate a study of his character with a study of his words. This is exactly what Dr Clifford Hill does. These studies are to be recommended for incorporating an analysis of the man alongside a contemplation on his message.' Bob Hunt, Vice-Principal, All Nations Christian College

PARDES

The Centre for Biblical and Hebraic Studies, also known by the Hebrew acronym Pardes, was formed in 1996 as a ministry at The Park. Its aim is to enable Christians to study the Bible from an Hebraic viewpoint so that they may obtain a better understanding of its message.

This is achieved by means of residential and non-residential seminars, teaching days, special events, correspondence courses, study tours, celebrations of Jewish festivals and a range of resources including publication of books, video and audio-tapes.

Please contact Pardes to request:

* information on the work of the Centre
* the free regular bulletin with news of events and resources
* information about current correspondence courses
* a resource catalogue
* details about teaching tapes
* information about Hebrew language tuition and resources
* a speaker to come to your area
* details of how you can help the work of the Centre.

Pardes may be contacted at:

The Park, Moggerhanger, BEDFORD, MK44 3RW, UK
Tel: (01767) 641007 Fax: (01767) 641-515
Email: pardes@the-park.net
Web: http://www.the-park.net

The Centre for Contemporary Ministry

The Centre for Contemporary Ministry (CCM) incorporates the Centre for Biblical and Hebraic Studies (Pardes); the Family Matters Institute and the magazine Prophecy Today.

CCM is based at The Park, Moggerhanger, a Grade 1 listed building which is being restored as a Christian Conference Centre and heritage site. It is responsible for operating The Park and plans to utilise it to host courses and conferences as well as opening it to the public for its historic interest.

In the 18th century, Moggerhanger Park was the country home of Godfrey Thornton, Governor of the Bank of England, who was linked to the Clapham Sect and cousin of William Wilberforce. CCM has a unique opportunity to show how Christianity has been at the forefront of our country's heritage and how Christians can make an impact in today's society through the various strands of our work.

Please contact us if you would like further details of any of our work or you would like to receive our regular newsletter.

CCM can be contacted at:
The Park, Moggerhanger, Bedford, MK44 3RW, UK
Tel: (01767) 641007 Fax: (01767) 641515
email: ccm@the-park.net
web: www.the-park.net